MY LIFE IN AGONY

MY LIFE IN AGONY

*Confessions of a
Professional Agony Aunt*

Irma Kurtz

ALMA BOOKS

ALMA BOOKS LTD
London House
243–253 Lower Mortlake Road
Richmond
Surrey TW9 2LL
United Kingdom
www.almabooks.com

First published by Alma Books Limited in 2014
This mass-market edition first published by Alma Books Ltd in 2015
© Irma Kurtz, 2014

Irma Kurtz asserts her moral right to be identified as the author of this
work in accordance with the Copyright, Designs and Patents Act 1988

Printed and bound by CPI Group (UK) Ltd, Croydon, CR0 4YY

ISBN: 978-1-84688-355-2
eBook ISBN : 978-1-84688-323-1

CONTENTS

1 – Who Do I Think I Am?   3

2 – Love is a Four-Letter Word   18

3 – Breaking up without Falling Apart   33

4 –The Family Business   50

5 – To Bear or Not to Bear   73

6 – Money Makes the World Go Round   92

    (And Doesn't It Go Fast?)

7 – Body Image Imagined   113

8 – Friends with a Feminine Ending   133

9 – Can Men and Women Be "Just" Friends?   155

10 – Snake-Belly Lows   178

11 – Truth and Consequences   201

12 – How Do I Know?   222

13 – Where Did I Put My Keys?   242

14 – I Told You So   264

MY LIFE IN AGONY

1

Who Do I Think I Am?

I was fourteen going on fifteen. I still pledged allegiance to the flag of the United States of America with my classmates, hands on hearts, at the start of every school assembly. It was a summer day in 1950, and my parents were doing a weekly stocking-up in the small town near our holiday home in the foothills of New York's Catskill Mountains. My little brother was indulging his incipient bibliophilia in the children's section of the local library under the eagle eye of the librarian, a woman never seen to smile, not even when she pointed to the sign "Bea Still" on her desk and warned new arrivals that it really was her name, so they had better not laugh aloud. I was sitting alone at the counter of the luncheonette in the main street. It was unusual to see a young person alone in a public eating place back then. It still is. Solitude in public looked like failure to us then – it felt like failure too. It still does. Unless – as in my case and that of others like me – to be alone came as a relief from wondering who we were and how we fit within our families and the crowd.

When another girl on her embarrassing lonesome walked into the luncheonette and stood for a moment in the doorway looking around, anxious and frowning, something told me she was going to make for the stool next to mine at the counter – never mind that plenty others were unoccupied, or even that she was at least three years my senior, which is time enough to put teenagers a world apart. She was dressed in fashionable "ballerina" style; I wore a shapeless skirt and a baggy blouse; her hair was "permanent-waved" to her shoulders, mine was in two thick braids nearly to my waist. In the mirror behind the counter I watched her wrinkle her nose when she saw the towering strawberry ice-cream sundae in front of me – and then, after an approving glance at her own reflection, she settled on the neighbouring stool: her skirt, over a starched petticoat, opened into an umbrella under her. Sometimes, when I recreate conversations and correspondence from the past, I invent the words, but I no more invent their themes and timing than I would of recollected music.

"I don't know what to do," she said in an accent like my own from the big city fifty miles to the west.

"The strawberry ice cream is yummy…" I replied, wistfully.

"Gimme a Coke," she said to the cute guy behind the counter.

He had been ogling her with a sparkle she did not return or appear to notice. I put my spoon down. I sighed. Only a beast would tuck into an ice-cream sundae while sitting next to a soul in confessional mode.

"It's my boyfriend. He says he's gonna stop going out with me if I won't do… 'it'…"

Her pauses underlined the significance of "it", and also made it clear that she had no more done "it" yet than I had. Virginity was not unusual among girls and young women of that time – on the contrary: it must have been common among our brothers too. The parents and teachers of my generation – quite a few of them born in the previous cen- tury – instructed us girls that to do "it" was all every boy wanted from any girl, and once she had done "it" with him he would have no more to do with her; nor would any other boy want damaged goods like her – not if he was a nice boy. Doing "it" was reserved for after marriage, and marriage was what nice girls were made for. The maidenhead was a gift and a burden we damn well better hang on to until we sacrificed it virtuously at the altar. All faiths, no matter how antagonistic they may be in politics and on the fields of war, are in accord to this day when it comes to rating virginity as a major component of every good girl's dowry.

"Do you want to do 'it' with him?" I dared ask the stranger, for I myself had recently begun to feel stirrings of physical desire, albeit no stronger than the tickling that precedes a sneeze.

Her grimace of horror wrinkled into disgust: "No! Of course I don't want to do it! My folks would kill me if I got pregnant!"

Nowadays teenaged girls are warned to beware of promiscuous intercourse because sexually transmitted diseases are reported to be on the increase in their generation; however, not only are such afflictions invisible on the dance floor, they are unimaginable to young people in throes of infatuation, and so STDs are a less effective deterrent to underage sex now than "getting knocked up" used to be. Procreation was the one and only reason adults gave us girls for doing "it"; later we would learn that it was also our duty to provide pleasure to the man with whom we were legally contracted, lest he stray away to find it elsewhere. Accidental pregnancy and a resultant baby labelled "illegitimate" were the hazard and punishment of unauthorized doing "it". Contraception was not to be had out of machines in the Ladies or over drugstore counters in those days: a diaphragm was the only defence available to girls, and to be fitted with one was a fiddly business involving lies and possibly the attempted forgery of parental approval.

"I don't know what to do," the stranger said yet again.

She stirred the straw around the glass in front of her; her fingernails were painted crimson. Had she and I been in the same year at the same school she would be one of the girls who jeered at my braids and lace-up shoes whenever we passed each other in the halls. But when she turned to me and I looked into blue eyes welling with tears, I could see it was not one like herself she needed now, it was not a friend she wanted: it was a listening stranger who had to be a female, one she was unlikely to meet again, who posed no risk of tattling to her classmates or her family. Should the stranger be able to offer her a spell or potion, so much the better; however, the most important thing for a troubled girl was to hear herself speak without interruption. And the moment this girl saw me plain and alone at the counter, she knew I would fill the bill.

"I'm crazy about him. He's crazy about me too. We're crazy about each other..."

"Crazy!" I thought. I only said: "If he cares about you so much, then why does he let himself make you unhappy this way?"

She frowned and, after a moment: "He gave me flowers for my birthday... "

"Flowers wilt and die," I thought, but red marks on exam papers had finally taught me that metaphor is often mistaken for obfuscation, so I said nothing.

"And he gave me gorgeous chocolates at Christmas..."

"Did he eat any of them himself?"

I anticipated her reply, and had asked the question only so she could hear herself answer it.

"He ate all the soft-centres," she said. Her scowl delivered a glimpse of the bossy, defensive old woman she would become some day, and the puzzlement of her tone flared into outrage: "He ate every last one of the soft-centres..."

The "soft-centre syndrome", in its less sexy, jelly-bean version, was already established in my beginner's Common Sense. Let a box of jelly beans appear in the sweets cupboard at home and my little brother was bound to scoff all the yummy red and orange ones with entitlement – unless, of course, I managed to get to them first.

"It isn't fair!" would cry whichever of us found only yucky greens and blacks left in the box. The black-and-green-jelly-bean syndrome taught me more about the selfish immediacy of appetite than any little virgin should have known, and observing it in action led me towards acknowledging animal appetites to be a challenge to courtesy and humane justice. Only our parents, who liked jelly beans too, always left plenty of the red and orange ones for my brother and me. So that must mean that fairness depended upon what? Fairness depended upon the triumph of generosity and self-control over hunger: love over lust.

"If he really loved you – if he really, really loved you – then he'd want to wait until you wanted to go all the way too."

In my mind's eye there flickered "The End" as it used to appear over a kiss – usually the first kiss – between the protagonists in the final moments of every black-and-white romantic movie of that era.

"To threaten to leave if you don't do 'it' is not nice: in fact, it stinks. It really stinks. It's a crime. It's blackmail. Your boyfriend is blackmailing you. And if you do 'it' because he blackmails you, then that makes you partners in crime. The crime of blackmail takes two, right? And then, even if you don't get pregnant, you're still going to feel guilty, right? And what if he goes and drops you anyway after you do 'it'? You'll think losing him is your punishment for doing 'it' with him."

I stopped talking and held silent for a moment, so she could sigh and nod a little.

"He's not thinking of you, you see? You've got to think of yourself, right? You have to decide what's good for you."

This time her nod was emphatic. She drained her Coke fast, dropped coins on the counter and exchanged a flashing look with the cute boy who had served her. Before she walked away and out of the door she mumbled a few words, certainly not "thank you": does a ventriloquist thank the dummy? I had merely spoken what she herself knew down deep and needed to hear aloud.

The next woman who entered alone into the luncheonette looked around for a moment, caught my eye in the mirror and hurried to take the empty place next to me. She was a grown-up, nearly three times my age: the wedding ring that had long ago been slipped onto her finger now pinched it into a sausage.

"My son never listens to a word I say," she began.

I pushed the ice cream to one side. Common Sense had been called into service. Like it or not, I was in business.

In the early 1970s, when I became a salaried "agony aunt" for the London edition of an international women's magazine, hesitant virgins were no longer two for a penny – nor even twelve for a shilling. And nowadays, the workaday agony aunt is hardly ever approached by fearful virgins of the parish. On the contrary, "All my friends are doing 'it' – what's wrong with me?" write today's teenagers inviolate.

"I don't want to get to thirty and still be a virgin," said a seventeen-year-old I spoke to the other day. "I feel like going with the next guy that comes along…"

Observant practitioners in a life of agony cease to be surprised to see that wherever an extreme exists, its opposite will be found not far away: wealth abuts on poverty, truth is an untold lie, love nudges enraged jealousy and friendship shares the table salt with envy – solid oaks cannot be separated from their shadows on the grass. So it is that problems ostensibly unlike each other can derive from the very same blip. To the impatient young virgin who contacts me now I say pretty much what I said to her hesitant predecessor of yesteryear: "Above all, do not have sex until you – and you alone are as sure as you and only you can be that you are prepared not only to enter a new area of frolic, but also to cope with a whole new source of potential misery."

Early agony aunts in printed broadsheets were in fact uncles. Whenever my journalistic niche is derided by snootier hacks, it eases the sting to remind myself – and them too – that back in the eighteenth century Daniel Defoe used to write advice pamphlets in which he opposed premarital sex, disapproved of abortion and divorce, and recommended no sex for women after the menopause. The brotherhood of "agony uncles" in general held themselves to be missionaries among the unknowing and immoral: they dealt in precepts and penitence, and they kept the screen of the confessional shut tight between themselves and the women who applied for help, lest they behold their female supplicants as unique and sexual beings.

We inveterate agony aunts do not descend from such stern ecumenical stock: we come by way of the old white witch who lived in a cottage at the bottom of the lane. Way back when the problems of the sexes were as disparate as their pleasures, the advice of those wrinkled and chosen spinsters was sought by women of the village, one on one. Her listening ear and her words were paid for in kind, not coin, as few women, even ladies of the manor, had cash at their disposal. Being distaff consultants meant that the old wise women could hardly go public in print until they and others of their sex were finally taught to read and write. Even after literacy was widespread, early advice columns on both sides of the Atlantic occupied themselves largely with genteel questions of etiquette. Only after the menfolk were called away to fight world wars – leaving the women to keep homes and homeland on even keels – only then did agony columns move from serviettes and fish knives into the deeper water of frustration and emotional tumult, where they have been bobbing around ever since.

It does not take long for a clever child to catch on to the fact that any piece of advice delivered by a grown-up is but a short hop from a command. Orders disguised as advice continue to be delivered to underlings first by parents, then teachers, employers, personal trainers, stargazers, palmists, hypnotists and shrinks too, who make their livings from purporting to know us better than we know ourselves. The genuine agony aunt is free from attachment to any ego-boosting faith or discipline: she has nothing to promote save her own commonsensical opinion of the case in hand. Otherwise, if she feels insecure without a structure more rigid than her own perceptions, she will probably set herself up as a counsellor or a therapist. The inveterate agony aunt never graduates from any school of thought: she keeps on learning.

So here I am with no letters after my name, no diploma in psychology on the wall: where do I get off giving unhappy strangers advice on their personal issues and behaviour? Who do I think I am? I am a purveyor of Common Sense. And Common Sense, though it has ever been endangered and these days it is muzzled by political correctness, continues to flourish mostly among us women, perhaps because its innate honesty does not sit easy with high position or over-weening worldly ambition. And it is women too who can become wise, whatever their level of scholarship. Wisdom is the apotheosis of Common Sense, its aim and its pinnacle. Common Sense moves steadily towards Wisdom by remaining non-judgemental and open to new ideas, even when they contradict old favourites. Common Sense and Wisdom work in tandem, but they cannot always agree, for they exist in different time zones: Common Sense is busy in the here and now, Wisdom recollects and foresees. Wisdom will always be older than Common Sense, for it must incorporate experience, evidence and observation during the long climb to a lonely point of overview.

During the heyday years of agony columns, a significant number of aunts in print were Jews: Marje Proops, Claire Rayner, Anna Raeburn in England and several more in America – all of them heiresses of the ghetto, where women practised pragmatic Common Sense as their brothers practised the fiddle: two portable instruments that could be carried on the next dash to safety.

The Jewish Daily Forward was a Yiddish newspaper published in New York from 1906 until the mid-1960s, with a vast readership composed largely of immigrants and their offspring. Its proto-agony column, called 'The Bintel Brief', dealt with practical and sentimental questions posed by members of families uprooted to a new land. To read 'The Bintel Brief' now is to eavesdrop on a sorority that was dedicated to arranging the matches of children, to making homes clean and kosher, and to keeping tabs on daily life in their "kitchen courts" while the menfolk were being high-toned and metaphysical in the "Rabbi's court".

"Love is sweet, but tastes better with bread!" goes one of the travel-worn and time-tested proverbs that were commonsensical cornerstones of 'The Bintel Brief' and of the kitchen court.

The future is a parade of possibilities waiting to strut on stage, should they be summoned. Natural cycles are preordained by nature; practically everything else we are or have or do depends upon our choices or on simple accident for shape and quality. We agony aunts deal with anxiety about choices – bad, wavering or regretted. The segregation of agony columns in women's magazines and in what were once called "the women's pages" of national papers has always placed us nose to nose with astrological columns, both slightly shameful sustenance for readers. To this day I watch young women on the underground shield their magazines or iPods and mobiles from the sight of neighbours while they smile to read that they are not the only ones who feel demeaned by a boyfriend's recourse to porn, say, or who suffer bitchery in the workplace.

And yes, before you ask, men do read agony columns too, on the sly.

"I know you. I've seen your picture over your column… I mean, like, my wife left the magazine lying around," a London cabby told me once. And then, as I've learnt to expect from similar encounters with men, he began: "I have this… uh… uh… like a friend, you know… uh… he… uh… well, he has a, like, a problem…"

Does Common Sense stumble on the road to Wisdom? You bet it does. Has the agony aunt had troubles of her own? You bet she has.

"A wise woman," says Wisdom, "is born asking for trouble."

"Do I take that as a warning?" asks youthful Common Sense.

"How you take it is up to you, youngster. Wisdom offers only the fact of what is the matter."

2

Love is a Four-Letter Word

"Dear Irma... we have been together for nearly a year. He is very caring and the sex is great. The only thing is, he has never once said he loves me. Even when I tell him that I love him there is silence. What's wrong? What should I do?"

"The man is scared. He's scared of his feelings for you as much and maybe even more than he's scared of your feelings for him. He's scared of being fooled or trapped by what he feels, if not by what you feel. For many people, especially male people, a declaration of love is hard to make, lest it be heard as the door slamming on freedom. The words 'I love you' will happen only when he knows himself ready for what they commit him to. He needs time; time to see that togetherness will not restrict his hopes, ambitions and possibilities; on the contrary, to be with you will strengthen him in every way. You're lucky that he is hesitant to say 'I love you'; some men and women too say it thoughtlessly, spurred by the moment, speaking more in hope than truth: they pave the way for pain. Of course you want to show how you feel about him in what you do and in the way you are. But wait before you say again: 'I love you'. Give him time to trust you, yes; even more to trust himself. And next time let him be the first to speak those words you want to hear..."

Like it or probably not, the guy has a point: "I love you" are spooky words. Every time you say them is the first time. Again. Repeat "I love you" to the same person night after night for a lifetime and it always carries a different intonation from any previous time you said it. Even if you hear "I love you" every day, each time it's as if you've never heard it before. "I love you": three little words immeasurable, they inspire waking and sleeping dreams, they can be freighted with devotion, with apology, with pleading and with anxiety. And "I love you" can be faked too, faked as easily to oneself as to the other, said more wishfully than deceitfully. And virtually overnight is "I love you" relegated by anger or despair to "I loved you". Then, you must wonder if a beautiful summer day dawned less bright and leafy because clouds gathered before nightfall? Was love a mistake because it did not last? Love is vast and phenomenal: it is central to family, to charity, to faith and to friendship. Without our ability to love, life would be a wasteland.

The moment Adam grabbed the apple out of Eve's hand, a schism opened between "love" and "falling in love" – whereupon men became a problem for women on earth, and even though men confide less fulsomely in agony aunts, or in anyone else, literature and history show that to be yet another vice that is often versa. Back when agony columns were known as 'Advice to the Lovelorn' and 'Lonely Hearts' columns, they addressed themselves to readers who could not find love or were not getting as much love as they wanted, or not getting it in the way they wanted. Nothing has changed in that department. If there were no love between the sexes and no manic lunacy of diving into it, agony aunts could go on long holidays.

And yet again is paradox growling under a general truth, for what is an agony aunt if not a purveyor of Common Sense? And to fall in love is to crash into a state of overheated obsession that is impervious to Common Sense. Only after the blaze has subsided and the apple has been digested, only after clear sight begins to function again, only then can Common Sense be heeded, and so at last love can emerge calm and stronger than ever out of the melodrama of "in love". Or maybe not, as the case may be.

In communities where women remain secluded from life outside the home, their youthful unions are arranged by elders, as indeed marriages used to be for us all, if more or less discreetly. There are societies to this day where the chance to stumble headlong into love is obviated, and should such a fall happen accidentally the result is dangerous, even fatal. Mortally disobedient love has come along in my life of agony; its potential for tragedy is so far beyond Common Sense or Wisdom that I am grateful there are courageous community advisors to whom I can safely refer it. Mind you, if stability and longevity and sheltered offspring were still our only requirements for a satisfactory relationship, with passion and equality and courtesy put to one side, my guess is that arranged marriages would top the league.

"Yes, my marriage was what you call 'arranged'. My husband and I know each other's families. We share a faith, we share traditions and we speak the same language. We have trust and we have children. Why should that not be love?" said the wife of my local newsagent, her accent as shimmering as her silken dress.

The shop door opened behind me. I turned to see her young-
est child, a beautiful girl of around seventeen wearing straight
jeans and a T-shirt emblazoned "Shock Value". I smiled hello
and asked what she was up to these days. Politely removing
her earbuds, she said: "I'm still a student."

"What are you studying?"

"Business Management."

Her mother winced and lowered eyes dazzled and frightened
by the alien present.

Among innumerable questions that come my way, there
has never been one, thank Goodness, concerning business
management. There has been one, however, just as unlikely:
it concerned football. My hairdresser was regaling me
with complaints about the way her boyfriend disappears
onto another planet whenever the team he supports is
playing.

"Last time they won – would you believe – he went out and
got drunk with his mates. He didn't come home until late
the next day. We nearly broke up over it," she said, snipping
scissors near my earlobe.

"I don't suppose," I said, rather hopelessly, "you could
develop an interest in football?"

"Don't be absurd," she replied – I was grateful it was only a comb she wielded now – "football is a game for the boys."

"A game for the boys": until not long ago sexual intercourse was a game for the boys. Women were encouraged to play too, but only as long as they stuck to rules applying to the female league. Not only was sex with the boys a dangerous game for women out of wedlock, but a depressing number of married women used to write to my column during the Seventies and Eighties because sex for them was but a joyless duty that kept the lock on wedlock.

Freedom is an ideal of Western life that women were allowed to share relatively late. To fall in love and into bed recreationally has only recently become one of the ways we women aim to enjoy our new freedom, and we are still often caught off guard by the risks entailed. Recreational sex, especially when it is blurred by drink and drugs, can end in misery that was undreamt of by those grannies and moms and aunts who fought for a woman's right to seek her own fulfilment. A woman now can act upon fanciful ambition or fall for those who pander to it; she can become subservient to fashion's regimented diets, to binge-shopping, drink, drugs or to a dimwit lifestyle endorsed by her favourite celebrity. And if she doesn't watch her step on the road to liberty, she will all too easily fall victim to a predator looking for easy pickings.

"I think I was raped…" is a morning-after line that comes my way – once would be too often.

"Rape is armed robbery not far from murder," I replied to one victim. "Rapists must be reported for punishment. But please, please remember that your new freedom to go out and play with the boys requires you to employ an even greater freedom, new to women, the greatest freedom we women have finally attained: the freedom at last to take responsibility for ourselves…"

"Irma Kurtz," shrieked an online critic after the letter appeared in print, "says rape is the victim's fault!…"

"You imbecile," I shrieked back, or would have done if online had an ear to shatter, "Common Sense must tell every young woman to exercise her new right to control herself and to be her own body's boss; let her never, never become a victim of the much lesser new freedom to get blotto in public. Rules of the road begin in the pub…"

How we fall in love and how we love are not exempt from fashion. The new way we use old words illustrates new ways of how we think and of what we wish were so. In my early days of agony, when a couple said they were "dating", it meant they went out in public together by prior arrangement, usually on Friday or Saturday night, when there was neither school nor work the next day. Around the late '80s, "dating" started to be a euphemism for "stringless" sex between two on an unofficial if regular basis. It was about the same time that "lovers" were shoved into poetic history by "boyfriends" and "girlfriends"; it was not going to be long before "live-in lovers" joined husbands and wives to become genderless and politically correct: partners.

"He's my new partner," whispered a female acquaintance while her companion was fetching drinks from the bar.

"Oh, well done…"

It was only when the man returned and told me that he was an architect I realized that my friend, who was a newly qualified solicitor, meant he partnered her in bed, not in a law firm.

"Waitresses" had been "servers" for a while before "actresses" woke up one morning to find themselves "actors", salesmen and saleswomen were suddenly "salespeople", "authoresses" became "authors" – even should their names be Jane or Emily. Only tigresses and lionesses and entitled nobility hang on to their proud endings – oh yes, and manhole covers too keep their gender to this day.

"Making love" has been overtaken by "having sex", impure and simple, never mind that whatever we make stands a chance of lasting lifetimes while anything and everything we have is over and done as soon as we've had it. However we put it, when things go wrong, believe me, heartbreak is no less now than it used to be when the "L" word ruled.

Not just words, but deeds too are subject to fashion and imposed opinions. Late in the 1970s, a number of women wrote to me genuinely worried about deriving no pleasure from the woman-on-top position. To be on top in bed was touted as an explicit metaphor for liberation, and so those who preferred not to straddle a penis feared they rejected feminist aims, or would be accused of it. Going by the flood of illustrated how-to books and brochures that arrive in my agony post, these days a cool female partner neither gives it nor takes it lying down; the favoured position, certainly the most photogenic when simulated for a camera, is doggie-style. Is that equality? Or does it mean that when it comes to the crunch the sexes still find it problematical to see eye to eye?

Common Sense en route to Wisdom keeps her eyes open: she weighs and measures a lot more than just her personal experience and her immediate responses. When it comes to, say, perfectly poaching an egg, expertise must be acquired through doing it, probably more than once. But when it comes to an agony aunt's response to another person's emotional and social issues, if it relies heavily on her personal experience, it takes a bossy, egocentric and not very helpful tone, which I'd call "matronizing". Common Sense lodges far from vanity, and Wisdom – if a woman is ever going to achieve it – requires non-judgemental acceptance of the individual addressing her as well as observation of what others are up to in her society. Of course a pinch of what the agony aunt herself has got up to in life must be one ingredient of her response, but it is never the recipe.

My imagined prince was going to rescue me from tedious conventions and my own innate dissidence. Eager as I was to be recognized as his soul's mate at first sight, it would have less to do with how I looked than with whom I was and how I thought. Aside from being clever and creative, he had to be bigger than I was, of course, or how would he sweep me up into his arms and carry me off on high seas of elsewhere and discovery? We would last our lifetime together, he and I, without ever marrying: I believed marriage to be a prosaic contract entailing a licence that relegated the wife to the passenger's seat. Marriage seemed to me demeaning to the passion of two who knew themselves destined to be one. Dedicated as I was to the pursuit of one love and convinced that he and I must some day find each other, I managed to fall in love constantly – or do I mean inconstantly? – and I never numbed to the pain of disappointment, not even when I was a grown-up and should have known better. Every time my heart was broken again, I told myself that the pain proved it was still beating. And as long as a heart beats, there is hope it will love again and at last, one day, be loved in return.

As for lust, until I was twenty it could not struggle out from under a quilt of romantic expectation. Besides, girls of my time were instructed in "the facts of life" by our bitterly amused mothers, who embellished them with warnings: must not, should not, damn well better not. Our brothers learnt their facts of life from daddy. Were the boys' facts the same as ours, I used to wonder. I still do.

My father opened the envelope from my secondary school. It contained the results of an IQ test to which all of us emerging adolescents had been subjected. He glanced at the enclosed paper, clicked his tongue and muttered: "Oy!"

"Did I pass, Dad? Did I fail?…"

"What does it matter? It would only go to your head."

"Isn't that where IQ belongs?" I thought, but young Common Sense knew better than to say it aloud. Instead, I said my customary: "Sorry…"

Intellectual curiosity and intelligence were not the least bit alluring in females of my time. Are they now? Have they ever been as sexy as a wiggle and big tits? Will they ever be? Endeavours measurable by a score, whether in goals or bank balance or IQ, turn us into competitive animals. And who falls in love with the competition? To do so threatens humiliation and self-defeat. Back in the 1960s and up until the early '80s guys referred to sex with a passing girl as "scoring". Not once in a long life of agony have I come across "to score" used by any woman in reference to her one-night stand. On the contrary, "Why has he not rung?" they used to ask plaintively after a one-nighter. And now they ask: "Why doesn't he text or email?"

My father was born into extreme poverty, where pennies glowed as gold. When I entered my teens, he removed me from expensive private education – "What's the point? You're a girl," he said – and enrolled me into a local "public" school. My little brother, on the other hand, remained in the smaller classes of fee-paying schools because, after all, one day he had to be a professional something or other and the breadwinner for a family of new Kurtzes. As a girl, I was bound to be supported under a different name by God only knew what nice guy would ever put up with me. I was a commodity – females were. And to this day every girl owes it to herself to work hard never, ever to be seen that way again.

"It's a man's world, Irma," mother warned me when she discovered that I had been sneaking out to visit the cafés of Greenwich Village, which was the local bohemia of my teenage days, where poets gave readings and Art was pronounced with a capital "A", and where I imagined my prince would turn up. Wisdom smiles now to recognize the man whose image can still sneak up on me and make me sigh – the man I never met and now never will, the man of my dreams: he is the renegade I myself would have been, had I been born a man and the world all mine.

Salt water rocked the dinghy. Douglas and I were alone under sail, beyond trees or rocks or roots or any heavy things. We had no destination in mind; we had no clock, not even a wristwatch between us. His hand was lean and tan on the tiller; his prematurely white hair, aglow in sunshine, won him the soubriquet "Silver Fox" on the Mediterranean island where we had met a fortnight earlier. Ten years my senior, Douglas grew up in Argentina before taking to the seas, so English was not his first language – nor was language his favoured means of expression: he made complex statements out of silver set with semi-precious gemstones. Half a century later, wearing a necklace Douglas made for me, I hear the following gulls and I can still see his eyes. I grew up among people with dark eyes that smouldered in the heat: it captivated me to watch his blue eyes twinkle. Love is said to arrive with the trill of a violin or the strum of a celestial harp – when I looked into my sailor boy's eyes and fell headlong into love, what I heard loud and clear was the shattering of glass.

The dream of love is born in every human breast, where it waits to be awakened. And dreams are in the realm of glass, created out of natural ingredients: they are fragile by design and vulnerable in a quake. Nevertheless, hand-blown bottles have been found in the tombs of the pharaohs; given attention and respect, dreams like glass can endure and even survive the dreamer.

Biologists tell us that birds laugh and fish cry, homosexual unions occur in species other than our own, and an organized family life exists among the four-legged. Only humans, however, are inspired by the dream of love to create music and images that fly to the heart. A pairing to make the first person for ever plural is part of our existential quest. And the dream of love made real has been know to hold two in unions that are glowing and translucent even when they are not transparent to outsiders. So if the young I, or any similar hopeful romantic, wrote to me now declaring her dream of one true love, I would not scold or scorn her, nor would I discourage her by recounting my own long history of disappointments. A quest is worth at least as much as its goal – and often it is worth more.

"Would you at least tell one like your young self to be a little more coy and careful than you were," chides my Common Sense. "And tell her to try harder to keep her wits about her this time, for Goodness' sakes!"

"More important than restraint or caution," says Wisdom to Common Sense, "and more important than her wits when it comes to love, wish the girl good luck."

3

Breaking up without Falling Apart

"Tell me, dear, does anyone at school ever ask you about your mom and dad? I mean, why we don't live together?" I asked my son.

I had not long before sold our little house in west London and downsized into two rooms that were set like shoeboxes, one above the other, in a bohemian area of central London. The profitable move helped me pay for my son's enrolment at a posh co-educational boarding school in Dorset.

"Oh Mum, you mean cos you two never got married? There are plenty of kids in my class whose parents are divorced. So what? But there is one annoying thing… Can you imagine, Mum," he said, sounding older than his fourteen years, "what I had to put up with when the guys found out what you do for a living?"

Even though the column I wrote for a popular women's magazine was classic "advice to the lovelorn" and very few out of every two dozen published problems dealt with specifically sexual problems and exercises, my occasional explicit responses were enough to elicit a nudge-nudge from passers-by who recognized me in the street or on public transport. So I guess some would say that I earned my son's school fees by employment as a sex worker in Soho. Of course, the genuine sex workers in our raffish neighbourhood never gave me a second look: it was I who goggled them on local streets, for I was full of curiosity about what they did and even more why they did it.

When I first moved to London's Soho, the window next to my desk overlooked the kitchen of a neighbourhood brothel. Two or three times a week I used to see a woman wearing a classic maid's uniform of black with a frilly apron – an outfit that suggested she must play a role in scenarios laid on for special clients when she wasn't washing dishes at the sink under the window across from my own. As hard as I tried to catch her eye, she would not look up from the sink: evidently she did not want the conversation I was hoping to have across the air shaft between us. And then one day the maid forgot to don her wig. She was a he. And so another drop fell into my collector's bucket, followed by yet another when he stroked his balding pate, and I could see a wedding band on his finger.

I was an early explorer in the uncharted territory of a woman's entitlement to go out on the hunt for her destiny instead of being assigned to it. We adventurers fell hard and regularly into love and then scrambled alone again and up the jagged wall out of it. All too often we thought wishfully that to be wanted by an attractive man was to be needed by him, and to want him was to need him. I was already deep into my thirties and holding my newborn in my arms before it came to me at last that wants are roused and satisfied in passing; needs, however, are far beyond impulse. Needs can last a lifetime with or without finding appeasement.

"The ideal relationship," says Common Sense, "is between two who continue to need each other."

"Right you are, girl," says Wisdom. "All ideals, including love, are ongoing pieces of work."

Whether a failing relationship explodes or drifts onto rocks, its breakup is hard on both partners, even if one of them longed for freedom and made a dash for it. Blame, guilt, anger and disappointment follow the end of a relationship, to say nothing of the expense of time and money too, often demanded by contract. Every partnership begins as a mutual investment, whether it is romantic or pragmatic, and investments are made with expectations of future returns, thus the collapse of a relationship is a mutual failure, no matter if the breakup is angry or relatively amicable, no matter how justified one ex may be in blaming the other. Emotional bankruptcy can be eased and will pass faster if insurance is in place before the business begins.

"I just turned thirty-three, he's four years older. I have a job I like a lot and I live in my own flat. We met six months ago at a friend's wedding and we have been seeing each other ever since. I really know this time he's the one for me. So why am I so hesitant about moving my stuff into his place like he wants me to? I really do love him. I just cannot make up my mind…"

"To feel sure you love him is one thing. To feel sure you want to change your way of life is another thing. How about talking over the idea of renting out your separate flats for a while and moving together for a specified term into a place that's new to both of you? That way you begin your partnership on even ground. And when your heart is in flight, do try to keep your feet on the ground, especially now that we women can tread the same ground as men. Whatever you decide to do, whether you stay independent or move in together, do nothing until the morning you both wake up as sure as you can be about the right thing to do…"

When it comes to relationships – as is true of life in general – it sets a good scene to hope for the best. Hope is an industrious virtue that inspires endeavour and keeps its eyes on shining goals. Wishful thinking, on the other hand, is a slothful indulgence: it fantasizes the desired outcome and then sits back believing it will happen. It must happen. Why? Because the wishful thinker wants it to happen. Hope keeps us brave and busy; wishful thinking turns us into ninnies.

The classic example of wishful thinking in my life of agony is the "other" woman attached to a married man who wishfully thinks he is going to leave his partner for her. And does he not think wishfully too? Did he not say he would? As soon as the kids are old enough. Or when the house is paid for. Or when his wife has recovered from surgery. Or the day daffodils bloom purple.

When a single woman complains about her married lover it is not in my remit or my nature to lecture her on morality. I can only warn her, first, of the threat her relationship with him poses to innocent others, and then of its greater threat to her own balance and self-worth. Dalliance with another woman's husband makes the other woman not so much a beloved as an accomplice. I wish I could show her the post-Christmas misery that arrives annually into my life of agony from mistresses upon finding themselves alone for holidays that even chronically unfaithful hubbies choose to spend with their primary families.

"He loves only me," once wrote one of many unhappy "other women". "He assures me there has been no physical relationship with his wife even before he met me three years ago. And he promises he is going to leave her as soon as their son is old enough to enter nursery school."

"It takes no more than simple arithmetic..." I begin my reply, until Common Sense reminds me that if wishful thinking knew how to add and subtract there would be no ruined gamblers on the breadline.

To love and be loved in return gives neither lover an excuse to abandon courtesy. On the contrary, partners in love are preternaturally vulnerable to each other's moods and behaviour. Naughty intimacy lets them drops the rules of etiquette along with their underwear by the bed. Courtesy, however, is much deeper and more personal than formal rules of etiquette. Courtesy embodies respect: a courteous partner allows the other opinions and priorities that are not his or her own. It is not discourteous to disagree; moods prevail and tempers are born to flare. But if a union is going to endure or if it will end without lifelong bitterness, contempt and mockery should keep their big mouths shut, sulks call time and fists stay in pockets, so when the noise or frigid silence abates "I'm sorry, my love" and "I forgive you, darling" can ring true.

Apology and forgiveness are the keynotes of courtesy. Passing infidelity is a serious discourtesy indeed, but it can be forgiven if not quite forgotten by a loving partner. Of course, enough is enough of good things too, and the point can arrive where serial forgiveness for serial discourtesies ceases to make betrayed partners heroic: it turns them into suckers.

Anyone free from thoughtless, knee-jerk optimism must note that sex is still more playful than pertinent to men in general, who take their own infidelities a lot less seriously than their partners do or would do if they found out about them. Of course women cheat too. Countless women in my long life of agony have confessed to guilt over an infidelity passing and often drunken. Their agonized communications generally end: "I love my partner. Should I tell him what I did?"

"No," is my unusually bossy reply. "Why hurt the one you love? Why stab his ego with knowledge of your betrayal? Could it be so he will punish you? And so assuage your guilt? If so, it won't work. Furthermore, it could start an ugly pattern of summoning his rage as evidence of love. Carry the guilt alone; let it remind you never to add to its weight – not drunk, not sober, not at home or abroad. Are you sure in yourself that the infidelity was a stupid misstep? Could it have been a reaction to something worrying in your primary relationship? If there is a problem between you and your partner, it will go away only if you face it and work on it together. In which case your infidelity was just a minor symptom or an avoidance tactic, still not worth discussing."

One brutal blow to a relationship can occur if the "other woman", mad for vengeance or resolution, contacts the wife of her ex to spill the boiling beans all over her. Because doing this hurts the man too, it has been known for the wife to find herself consoling her husband after her own enraged pain has subsided and his abject apology is eventually accepted. In two cases of discovered marital infidelity that I have encountered among my own acquaintances, the union actually resumed on a footing stronger than before. And in the third, the double-crossed wife, now ex, and the jilted mistress became great chums.

"He was vain and hopeless," is how my friend explains their unlikely friendship, "but he had great taste in women."

"Unfaithful" – the word shudders in the ear, a dirty concept that sounds virtually criminal; otherwise how could it be the sustaining element of scandals and the sheets reliant on them? Infidelity gone public has been known to demolish a man's prestige overnight, for it usually is a man who falls from high esteem, even if his betrayed wife hangs on beside him after his shenanigans have been revealed. If he is able to cheat his partner out of her investment of hope and dignity, how can the rest of us trust him with our money or our votes of confidence? Flashy though infidelity is in the courts and readable in the press, when it comes to destroying relationships, arrogance, stinginess, detachment, bad temper and similar ongoing discourtesies on both sides are just as effective and even more common. Explosive episodes of sexual jealousy are unexpectedly common too, without anything to go on beyond the chronic insecurity of the jealous partner.

"If he so much as talks to another woman, it's hard to stop myself making a scene. My last relationship broke up because of my jealousy, and I am scared that it's going to ruin things again..."

"You know that your jealousy is unfounded and illogical, so your own lack of self-worth must be where it originates. Why should you feel unworthy of the dedicated affection of one who chooses you to be his companion? Is there an unhealed wound in your past? A scar you fear to let him see? Or even to see yourself? If there could be, then get to work on it. Start creating reasons to feel pride in yourself. A new language, a new skill, a charitable endeavour, a line of study, or even just a new look can work towards restoring a shaken self-image. Cultivate yourself, not to hold his interest – that's up to him – but to keep you interested in yourself. And by the way, be warned that unjustified jealousy can create its own justification when he starts to think, if he must endure false accusations, why not earn them..."

My life in agony was barely mature before I started to hear horrified screams arise from women upon discovering their partners' collection of porn – usually in the glove compartment of the car, the garden shed or the garage. One friend told me she found her boyfriend's dirty stash between the covers of Volume 16 of the *Encyclopaedia Britannica*, which he had hollowed out to hold it beside his desk.

"The volume that begins with Napoleon," she said, no smile on her tear-streaked face. I faked a cough to cover mine.

Her pain derived as usual from the idea that she was not "enough" for his satisfaction – or why did he need air-brushed fantasies?

"Can't you consider the stuff to be a snack?" I asked her. "Like a packet of salted nuts, say, he nibbles between banquets with you? And then, if you feel you must tell him what you found, you could say you'd like to tuck into the peanuts with him. Who knows? You might find them tasty to share…"

Porn has been around since prehistoric wall-painting: only recently has it moved online with the rest of the entertainment industries. Online porn wiggles and thrusts and is more successfully voyeuristic than words and frozen pictures, more personal, less gregarious than strip clubs and pole-dancing. It provides shallow triumphs in secret; being constantly available it is easily habit-forming and would be as trivial as online solitaire except that cyberspace is densely populated: breathing people in front of screens can share sexual or romantic fantasies with breathing strangers at their own screens.

And thus does relatively innocuous porn begin to approach infidelity. Cybersex and steamy chat-room flirtations are causing every day more incidents of jealousy in established partnerships. During the past techno-decade innumerable women have discovered a partner to be involved not just sexually, but romantically too, with a fantastic avatar he has never actually met. Because such a discovery entails snooping into his files, it suggests suspicion before evidence. It also makes puzzling his careless neglect of the "delete" button. Why does a man risk being caught, if not quite *in flagrante*, not far out of it? Does he need his partner's jealousy to boost tremulous self-confidence? Does he hope the discovery will heat up her competitive performance in bed? Or does he want her to bully him out of his addictive porn habit?

"Choose any of the above," says Common Sense.

"And then," says Wisdom, "choose all the others."

Decades before the island of Ibiza became urban spillage in the Mediterranean, weekly boats from the Spanish mainland were the only way to get there. I arrived on a fortnight holiday from penury in Paris and ended up staying for more than a year thanks to the blue-eyed sailor from Argentina who was standing dockside when my boat landed, waiting for me – or so we thought when we saw each other for the first time.

The only hang-out catering to foreign visitors back then was in the port town. The Domino Bar was run by a good-looking womanizing Englishman and a solemn Canadian who said little and drank less. Their establishment occupied a basement that was several steps down from the pavement, so it was perpetually dark as midnight. Old regulars perched on stools set around a semicircular counter; the English owner made himself one of the crowd and the quiet Canadian saw to the till, while a local barman served drinks and stoked the record player out of a stellar collection of vinyl American jazz. It was not long before I noticed that when Douglas and I appeared at the top of the stairs the music would stop suddenly and the barman replace whatever tune had been interrupted with some heartbreaking song by Billie Holiday.

Douglas used to shrug and smile down into the dark room. My dazzling leap into love made me slow to take note of the glaring brunette who appeared to be permanently installed at the far end of the bar. One evening Douglas told me at last that she had been his girlfriend until I came along. It was she who had been slipping the barman a nod, and probably a few pesetas too, to switch on the lovelorn tune whenever her ex and I made an appearance.

"Sexual jealousy is inflammable and it can be dangerous," Common Sense observes. "It has committed plenty of murders in human history."

"So thank your stars, Irmele," says Wisdom, "the only weapon your jilted predecessor had to hand was an old phonograph needle."

When a relationship runs into trouble, chances are that both partners know down deep whether or not it can be saved, and they both must want to save it too, if it is to get back on keel. Every couple creates their own chemical blend, which is as unique as either of its components. There are some couples, for example, with a mutual dynamic dependent on quarrels that are fiery and genuine, sometimes entailing a weep on the shoulder of a local agony aunt, who will finally learn to say nothing after she notices that the sequential spats are always followed by sexy making-up again.

"Whatever works for a couple must add up to a good relationship," says Common Sense.

"Until they multiply," says Wisdom.

As soon as offspring appear, the balanced and established pair needs to accommodate the newcomer. It can happen that upon the arrival of a baby, for reasons usually more physiological than logical, a new mother temporarily loses interest in sex – which is mistaken by the partner as her old interest in him swallowed by her new interest in their baby. Once again, patience and communication are urgent to allow, first, a settling-down of bubbling maternal hormones and then a reorganization of responsibilities and timekeeping in order to rebalance a partnership which has become a corporation. Our increasing divorce rate suggests that fewer unions feel they must stay united "for the sake of the children", as troubled marriages used to do and still did when I began my life in agony. Is forsaking "the sake of the children" progress in the history of matrimony? Sometimes it probably is. Children have ever been the victims of battling or neglectful households. Plenty of offspring of earlier generations would have been better off in the long run had warring parents been able more easily to split and learn to love them separately. Breaking-up is never a happy decision; sometimes, however, it is the only one.

The third-floor studio flat in Paris was barely wider than our bed – which was now all mine. My bed stood in an alcove to the left of the entry. From then on I was going to struggle to tug it out alone whenever the sheets required changing, presumably less often now that I would sleep alone. The room was less than the length of an underground carriage, on its far side were five bookshelves nailed high up on the wall over a table and, opposite, a single wide shelf, "the kitchen", holding a basin and a hotplate. At the far end of the room was the only window, floor-to-ceiling: it looked out on a church built in an earlier century; its chimes would hereafter tell me alone the passing hours. Through the open window flowed an aroma of the fruit of the day being puréed by the *sorbetière* across the street: blackcurrants on Monday, apples on Tuesday, oranges on Wednesday, pears on Thursday and lemons on the weekend. I stood in a citric miasma to watch the other half of our first-person plural leave me. He did not look up, only doubled his height into the back of the car that was being driven off to Spain by two of his friends – once ours – returning to the island where several years earlier Douglas and I had become an unofficial "we".

Life in Paris had turned out to be feckless and unbearable for my seafaring man, while for me any time spent on the Balearics could not be more than a holiday. Love each other? Yes, we loved each other for a while. But neither of us liked the person he or she must become if we were to stay together. The car pulled away down the narrow street, and I gasped at the slash rendering us back into me.

"Ending us hurt like hell," reminds my Common Sense. "It put you out of commission for a while."

"But ending 'us' wasn't the end of you, was it? The agony of ending 'us' tested your determination to discover your singular self."

"Don't you mean *invent* yourself?"

"Six of one," Wisdom replies, "and half a dozen of the other," say Wisdom and Common Sense in chorus.

4

The Family Business

Our first contract is a birth certificate. Mine was validated by a three-inch footprint: my newborn fingerprint must have been too tiny to serve in evidence that this newcomer had begun her life's employment in the human conglomerate, specifically attached to Company Kurtz – at least for twenty years or so, until as a female I would be expected to sign a new contract changing my name and affiliation to a subdivision in the massive industry of procreation. Home and housekeeping would thereafter be my life's work in exchange for room and board provided by the boss. Respectful love was required too in the agreement undertaken between new twosomes in the hereditary business, and fidelity was guaranteed by the contractual clause specifying "obedience" only from the female signatory: how else, pre-DNA testing, could the validity of her offspring's claim to enter the paternal dynasty be assured? Carrying new life into existence is upfront, long-term and visible; to sire the baby takes but a passing moment. Or a passing stranger.

When I was a child, America was still nirvana for Europe's huddled masses. My family lived on the East Coast, near the seaports of arrival; the immigrants who had settled in our neighbourhood hung on to their heirlooms of taste and tradition nowhere more evident than in the kitchens of my classmates' homes, some laid out in strict kosher pattern, others with bottles of golden oil and pots of basil on the window ledge, and a few redolent of spices – saffron, curry, tamarind – to inspire dreams in a nascent traveller. Women sat at their kitchen tables peeling vegetables while they chatted in languages that were fading among their American-born children. Before media took control of domestic entertainment, the family furnished its offspring with myths and melodies and bedtime stories handed down through generations. Propagation of political affiliations too have always made the family unit strategic to politicians as inherited religions make it central to ecumenical establishments. Government-supported and faith-based, the old family business is bred into our very bones. Of course there are rebels and dropouts from the ancient order: I became one of them the first time I heard salt water lapping my natal coastline and whispering tales from beyond the horizon.

A woman born for a life in agony soon notices how haphazard are the demographics of strangers who confide in her, how embossed by vanity and contorted by wishful thinking is what they declare and want to believe as fact. Thus, a traveller on the road to Wisdom learns to take all published statistics pertaining to our emotional and sexual lives with grains out of the sack of salt that Common Sense keeps ever to hand. Unsalted statistics are regularly published to tell us that marriage is on the decline – and yes, the word "marriage" does appear infrequently in modern agony's correspondence. However, I have yet to open one postbag or inbox that does not bulge with longings for a "partnership" and anguish about "commitment" – usually phrased: "Why won't he go for it?"

To which Common Sense has more than once had to reply: "Why should he?"

Not very long ago the word "commitment" referred to incarcerations a lot more restrictive than marriage. Whether or not a formal and binding contract of marriage is signed before witnesses, the promise of exclusive togetherness – commitment – is always anticipated, certainly by young women. We are animals too, after all, driven to procreate and then to shelter our babies through one of the longest childhoods in nature. Being sophisticated critters with ideas above a furry, four-legged station, we use our intelligence and gift for invention to adapt nature to our pleasure and profit, or simply to squeeze it into current fashion. Nevertheless, one way and another, the basic concept of sexual partners contracting together for life stays rooted even while it bends in shifting winds.

It was back in the 1960s that the hippies decided to scramble nuclear families into one big apolitical jumble. Their short-lived experiment in communal living remains dark and dismal in the collective recollection of all its women and offspring I have encountered over the decades. One of many drawbacks to loving en masse is that pregnancy and lactation puts females *hors de combat*, while putative daddies go on merrily disseminating their semen.

Among the alternatives to monogamy that have crossed my path, only polygamy has a sturdy history, albeit peripatetic and faith-based. A sensitive nose in the suburbs of Salt Lake City is stung by mouldering melancholy that still emanates from little white cottages – two, three, four in a row – designed in the past by Mormon husbands as mirror images of each other right down to identical patterns on their twitching curtains, lest outbursts of sexual jealousy that were forbidden among the wives of a shared provider seek to disguise itself under envy of the taller chimney or bigger bedroom of another wife's house.

The notion of partnership that comes my way in a life of agony is more romantic these days than ever before, more love-based, less overtly pragmatic than it used to be when women moved from papa's home straight into hubby's home. Modern families produce fewer children than they used to do, and they less often include their older generations at the hearth. The aged are a burgeoning agony to themselves and their children now that there is no more surplus of daughters so that one of them can be tacitly designated to remain a spinster and undertake parental care in due course. Small though our families have become, they continue to demand conformity within the walls of home, and thus they arouse dissidence, more than ever now that daughters can be dissident too.

"My mom and dad would kill me if they knew..." forty years ago was an everyday line used by a young woman in agony as a prelude to anything from the loss of her virginity to her lust for another girl or for an outlandishly priced handbag. Gradually, it dropped out of the catchphrases of agony to be replaced by filial anger at parental interference

and contempt for their expectations. One of the most important freedoms new to women, although hardly yet the most
exercised, is our emerging freedom to be honest – honest at
last, each of us honest about her hopes, her opinions and her
appetites – honest first of all with herself: only then can she be
honest with others. Honesty is the lynchpin of independence
in the vast new world of choices, and yes, it can weigh heavy
on family life, because honesty often entails rebellion. What
great freedom has not needed rebels to fight for its inception
and its survival?

"I'm going to be a nun," Anne told me.

Anne and I were barely into our teens, so "when I grow
up" no longer needed to be uttered aloud. Anne was the
first-born in a family of seven with another perpetually
on the way, and all but the penultimate thus far were girls.
After twenty years in America, her parents still spoke with
an Irish lilt. They lived year-long in a clapboard cottage
across the street from the holiday home my family used for
school holidays and fair-weather weekends. Anne's father
commuted to the city for his work and was rarely to be seen
at home except after nightfall and on weekends. Anne and
I were sitting side by side on the dock, lakeside, watching

our siblings splash in the water; we could not frolic with them, because our menstrual periods had begun, so we were both sealed in bulky swaddling. Tampax was new on the market then, and not recommended for a good girl lest it damage the hymen and put her virginity under suspicion on her wedding night.

"If I were a boy, I'd be a priest," Anne said. "But the folks have only got Jamie. So I'm going to be a nun. I have the calling. My mom says I do."

In spite of being a certifiable adolescent, I was sometimes childishly literal-minded, and thus I was tempted by the occult: literal thinkers are attracted to make-believe to enliven the tedium of seeing everything as it really is.

"The calling, Anne – what does the calling sound like? Is it like a song? Or is it an order?"

"It's not that kind of calling. It's a different kind of calling. I sort of feel it," she said, and hearing herself sound dubious she added firmly: "My mom says so."

Anne was already buxom; her pale skin freckled in sunshine as fast as mine tanned; before she turned her eyes of mossy green away from me, I glimpsed someone much older behind them – someone who was scared. "My mom says it's meant to be."

I did not envy Anne her obedience, nor did I envy her a calling, for I expected some day to hear one of my own. I envied Anne nothing – nothing much – only the golden cross dangling between her new breasts. How I would have liked an amulet of my own to wear in defence against the assault of adolescence!

"But don't you want to travel, Anne? To see the world?" I asked, for these were starting to be my own priorities. "And don't you want a – you know – a boyfriend? And what about – well, you know – babies and all that?"

Anne's right hand twitched in her lap: was it resisting the urge to rise in the sign of the Cross? "I'm going to be the bride of Christ."

"But Christ already has brides, Anne – lots of them. I see them walking in the city. They go out two by two in long black robes. And they're locked up every night, aren't they? It can't be much fun…"

"You're jealous," Anne said, anger scratching her words. "You're jealous because you can never be a holy sister. You know why? Because you killed Him, that's why. The Jews killed Christ."

She was on her feet, calling out to her siblings that it was time to go home.

"We'll see – we'll see who'll be wearing black," she said to me over her shoulder, "on the Day of Judgement."

Five years later, on a dazzling September morning, a few days after my return from a student tour to Europe, I crossed the road outside our country house to deliver a gift for Anne. Her mother, a stout and faded version of her oldest daughter, opened the door to my knock; she examined the rosary I handed her and appeared to be counting the beads while I told her how I had bought it in Rome and held it above my head for a public blessing by the Pope in St Peter's Square. The latest and probably the last baby started to cry in the background – yet another girl, this one called Bernadette, referred to by my mother as "burden and debt".

"Is Anne happy in the convent?" I dared to ask as her mother was turning away.

She paused for a moment to reply over her shoulder: "What daughter of mine would not be happy to serve the Lord?"

My brother and I used to watch Anne's father layer his family into their old Ford for the drive to Church every Sunday morning. They never piled into the car on Saturday night as we did to go watch a movie at the drive-in cinema. My Eucharist was 7 Up and popcorn, my sacrament ended with "happily ever after"; romantic love presented itself to me on a black-and-white screen as the ideal destiny and the closing kiss as a blink of eternal life. True love, love beyond "The End", love but once and for ever brought a girl security and completeness of soul that seemed not all that different from the promise of the convent – except, of course, the holy sisters were spared the troubling mysteries of sex.

Psychoanalysis was becoming a cult and status symbol when I entered Columbia University in 1952. "Shrinking" was touted among the affluent as a cure-all for angst and aggravation. One avant-garde women's college even required all its incoming students to undertake a year of psychoanalysis whether they needed it or wanted it, whether they liked it or not. My own bluestocking college made no such requirement, however: groups of us used to gather in the girls' dorm for spontaneous seminars that always began as scholarly chit-chat and then frequently turned into sessions of competitive family-bashing. The analysands – who were also the richest girls among us – used a bash-and-blame vocabulary that left us, the great unshrunk, gawping. Words they laid out on the table – megalomania, psychoneurosis, preconscious cathexis, Electra and Oedipus – were as tempting as chocolates, and as hard not to gobble.

"My parents have a subconscious investment in sibling rivalry," said the second-year student to the dozen or so of us crammed into her small room for what had begun as a discussion on the Romantic poets. "They think they're boosting my brother's masculine confidence by questioning everything his sister does – i.e. every last thing *I* do. I bought tulips for Mom's birthday, and she actually said I did it to shame my brother. Of course he'd forgotten it was her birthday. Everything I do is a displacement exercise, according to her…"

"I have a confession," interrupted the tall girl sitting on the rug next to me. "I have to confess that even though I've asked you all to call me Alice, the name on my birth certificate… it's actually Alfreda. My dad is called Alfred, see? And my shrink says to name me Alfreda is clear evidence how much my folks hoped their first-born would be a boy. Alfreda! Can you beat that?"

"I can beat that," I heard myself say. "I was the first child too. And recently I came across the letter my mom sent to her mom, who was still living back in Indiana when I was born. 'It's a girl,' Mom wrote – and then in brackets: 'Drat it!'"

Common Sense was learning that truth can be boldest told if it is played for laughs: after a heartbeat pause, I punched the line: "A daughter wasn't worth a damn!"

The room was silent. One girl – her father happened to own a bank – scribbled the name and number of her analyst on a scrap of paper and passed it to me.

"Dear Irma," wrote a worried girl back in the early '80s, "my boyfriend's dad has a girl on the side, and I'm really worried infidelity could be in my boyfriend's genes…"

"Should the problem arise in your relationship," I replied, "believe me, it will be in his jeans, not in his genes…"

The pragmatic function of a family is as a delivery van: long after the youngsters have disembarked, they continue to blame every hiccup and setback on its dodgy brakes or its sluggish transmission, on windscreen wipers that never worked, or because the bloody thing broke down altogether. Having decided upon something – or, better still, someone – to blame for what ails them, many a woman (and plenty of men too) believe the problem to be as good as solved. Bar the shouting. However, blame – including self-blame – is befuddling, wallowing and self-justifying, and distracts energy from forgiveness and acceptance and finding solutions. As far as babies know, and some never learn better, they are born unto gods all-powerful. Plenty of their parents would agree with them. And so does blame

root and flourish within the family where loving acceptance is blighted by approval on one side and confused with
obedience on the other.

My parents were dismayed when I declined postgraduate
study and chose instead to return to Paris and recover my
dreams from the smoky Latin Quarter cafés, where I had left
them while on my student tour. I could expect no support for
an eccentric project that would remove me from my homeland
and the local marriage market, so to finance my exodus I had
to bunk at home with my scowling parents while working long
shifts as an over-educated waitress in a Midtown restaurant.
Dressed in my server's uniform, I observed fetishes at table
that were every bit as revealing of human fears and fantasies
as any practised in bed.

"Are there tomatoes in the *salade niçoise*?" asked the sub-
urban housewife. She was lunching with two friends: their
shopping bags, with contents worth a hundred times my
weekly wage, were piled on the floor around their chairs.
"I'm allergic to tomatoes," she said. "And I want lemon in
the dressing – no vinegar: vinegar makes me nauseous…"

An experienced waitress could predict what was going to
come next as surely as she knew that no male customer was
going to order artichoke for a starter, and pre-prandial whisky

drinkers went for beef as a main course, with fish or chicken favoured by the gin-and-tonic brigade.

"I'll have the *niçoise* too," said the companion on her left. I waited before scribbling her order on my pad to allow her time to say: "I want the eggs scrambled on the side, not hard-boiled. Hard-boiled eggs," she proclaimed to the table at large, "are indigestible."

"Is your cheese omelette made with gooey Swiss cheese?" asked the last in the trio.

Producing a smile out of my empty wallet, I said that yes, the cheese was Swiss.

"I want mine with American cheese. And boiled potatoes, no fries for me…"

Common Sense recollects fussy orders from the menu as symptomatic of the *faute de mieux* – "better than nothing" – syndrome that affects women to this day. A failure of control over big issues – money, love, sex and status – can make us obsessively controlling of little things within our reach. While serving the salads and omelette, I wondered how often the little things within a woman's dominion include her children.

It came as no surprise later in my life of agony to find that complaints about mamas, step-mamas, mamas-in-law – and sisters too – outnumber by far those concerning dads, who are blamed for detachment and abandonment but rarely for active meddling, except when they disapprove of a daughter's suitor. Undoubtedly the agony of sons, were they to speak of it, would more often be father-orientated with a base in competitive ambitions.

No matter how radically changes the design of the modern family, it takes a long, long time for its members to see each other as unique and vulnerable individuals, if indeed they ever do. Wisdom smiles ruefully to note how rarely Mama or Papa or both are credited to have got much right, and so they can remain a lifetime target of offspring's facile blame.

Agony postbags swell on the far side of Christmas after far-flung kin have returned home for celebrations that ended in sulks and tantrums. Upon family members' arrival, they find old grudges, jealousies, childhood idiosyncrasies and guilty secrets waiting for them under the tree, where they all deposit the ones they have brought along, wrapped and polished for the occasion. On an invisible rack hang the costumes ready to be squeezed into again: black sheep, shining hope, piggy in the middle – and there will be a cloak and dagger too, for the annual performance of family drama needs a villain or two.

"I'm a language teacher. I am married and I have a beautiful ten-year-old daughter. Why does my mom always put me down when the family gets together? Our family Christmas always ends in a fight. This year I went ballistic when I heard her tell my little girl in front of everyone not to listen to one word I said! She treats me as if I were the naughty teenager I used to be. Why can't she see I'm grown up and give me the respect I deserve?"

"Maybe your mother fears losing power and control, and so her heart drags her back to when you were a child and she was securely in charge not only of you, but of herself too. Whatever the reason, she does not know how to grant you mature status – or she dares not. So you'll have to grab it for yourself. Be mature. Show adult patience instead of adolescent anger. Count to ten, smile and give a wink to your little girl, so she sees it as a joke that your mother treats you as a little girl too. Behave as a grown-up and, in due course your mum will be persuaded to treat you as one. And if she never manages to grant you maturity? So what? Christmas comes but once a year: someone has to make it merry. Let the angel be you…"

Terminal versions of the holiday drama are launched when parents die and instead of harmonic eulogy all hell breaks loose grave-side.

"My kid brother completely ripped off Mom and Dad," snarled a friend of mine, newly orphaned in his fifties – and he added paradoxically, or so I assume: "My brother's a bastard!"

Whereupon he hurled himself into the impassioned bookkeeping that is all too familiar – not to say familial – among ageing orphans who want to build screens of material inheritance thick enough to hide their agonizing suspicion that the other or others were more loved and wanted by Mom and Dad.

"Why don't you open a dialogue with your kid brother?" I asked my friend. "Nothing else can lead to peace between you."

"Easier said than done," he snapped back.

"I dare him or you or anyone," Wisdom whispered in my ear, "to name anything worth doing that is not easier said."

There is not all that much in life we cannot choose or refuse, begin or end, alter or destroy: only the family we are born to is immutable. Which is not to say that siblings have the same childhood: not even identical twins recollect from a viewpoint of identical personality and experience. Only between and among themselves can brothers and sisters assemble the multidimensional portrait that is their mutual inheritance, the point and purpose of a family, whether it is happy or not. If the antagonistic ageing siblings I come across in my life of agony would only dedicate a little energy and intelligence to repairing their broken links, they might discover an unexpected source of comfort during lonely patches of the journey, a support over the bumps and a once-in-their-lifetime intimacy that can exist only by way of blood.

"You know, Irm," said my brother on one of our transatlantic phone calls, "I saw Mom angry loads of time, but I never once saw her cry."

"I did, Mook, only once. It was after Dad's funeral. Mom and I came home together from the cemetery in a taxi. I had barely unlocked the front door and, before I could even step back, Mom pushed past me. She hurled herself on the carpet. She was shrieking; she was gasping and shrieking. I went to hold her, but she shoved me away. All I could do was wait until the shrieks and sobs subsided. She asked me for a coffee, and by the time you and the others arrived, it was as if nothing had ever happened. I remember seeing Dad cry once too. He stood in the doorway to the kitchen. 'FDR just died!' That's what he said, and he began to cry real tears. I must have been about five – maybe six? I never forgot it."

"Gosh," my brother said, "now I won't ever forget it either!"

On our two sides of the world time stood back to let our parents take a bow. It was too late for apologies or explanations, but not too late for understanding and forgiveness – forgiveness of our parents, yes, and of ourselves too for not having understood sooner that they were "only" human. It was not too late to welcome into our hearts the love that is born indebted.

"Your father…" my mother used to say with a sneer directed by inference at me, as I was the first to have made a father of him. "Your father…"

Their battles about everything and nothing a child could comprehend were followed by long, impenetrable silences a lot scarier than their shouting.

"Never get married," mother used to warn me.

"Your mother is turning you against me…" my father used to say.

Only years and years later, after I dismantled my own battle stations against both of them, did Common Sense sigh to acknowledge that they both had a point.

It was a few weeks after Mother died in her nineties and I was sorting through the detritus of my parents' lives with a heavy heart when I came upon a sepia photograph of my father, tall and dashing in his youth. It was then, as I looked into the image of his dark, dreaming eyes, that I realized his outbursts of anger beginning at the time of my adolescence were not in fact directed at me. Men are romantics of great style, and one of their classic roles is as protector of the beloved. My father was afraid: he feared that his little girl's inexperience and curiosity would make her prey to pirates. My father was afraid for me. And fear makes men angry primarily at themselves for feeling afraid. My father's anger, followed by frozen silences, happened whenever I said or did something that threatened him with trembling on my behalf.

Now, I hold a picture of Mother, a beautiful girl, her hair cropped in flapper fashion. An only child living in a Midwestern flyspeck of bigotry, mother was barely walking when her father died of tuberculosis and left her to be raised by her mother and maternal grandparents, my great-grand-parents, immigrants who spoke English with an accent and Hungarian between themselves until, after one spectacular quarrel, they never again spoke another word to each other. Love was a silent instrument in my mother's childhood; she relied on make-believe to enliven her solitude. Petite and pretty, she was clever too, and chosen to attend the state university, which was an uncommon achievement for a girl of that place and generation. It was there she met the handsome New Yorker, a dental student twelve years her senior, and her energetic imagination got straight to work on a journey out of the hinterlands, off to the glamour of the East Coast and happily ever after. What would I have replied had Mother been able to consult me in my capacity of Agony Aunt?

"Dear Myra, he is the first of six brothers and two sisters, and his parents are orthodox Jews. He had to help support his younger brothers through their education before he could train for dentistry. It was not his first choice of profession, by the way, and became a lifelong disappointment. True, he was born in New York, but Jersey City is where his family lives now. And so will you, right next door to his mom and dad. Jersey City may be barely a mile on earth from the Manhattan skyline, but it is a million miles away in dreamland. So, before you give your heart, please wait and think and know a little more…"

And thus might Common Sense have done my brother and me out of existence.

The palm-sized cardboard discs I take up next are joined by a silken thread with a broken pencil dangling from its loose end. On the upper disc is printed: South Grove Commencement Dance, June 6th, 1931, and beneath it is my mother's signature, Myra Auerbach, written in her contrary backhand. On the second disc, under the heading "Dances", are two columns of spaces numbered one to ten with my father's initials pencilled in all of them. And at the bottom in his rhythmic forehand is written: "Every dance, my darling, forevermore!"

The card it is that dances before my eyes, and I can hear my father's strong, true tenor: "Somebody loves me, I wonder who..." while he stamps up and down the hill beside our country house pounding fresh snow underfoot so my brother and I can belly-flop on sleds down a crisp and even slope. I close my eyes for a moment, and mother's voice begins: "Once upon a time there was a little girl who talked to butterflies..."

Stories that mother made up held my brother and me and all our playmates in the palm of her hand: games and rituals flowed from her genius sorcery.

Yes, my parents were quarrelsome and not for long a happy pair. And yes, a greater investment of their aspirations was in the boy than me. Nevertheless, my brother and I were equal beneficiaries of their love, as I know at last in retrospect. And where does childhood end if not in retrospect? As is true of every other prejudice, memories of our families must be up for constant review.

"The only mind you can ever count on changing," says Common Sense, "is your own."

"And the mind that cannot change," adds Wisdom, "has ceased to think for itself."

5

To Bear or Not to Bear

Before Skype and Facebook, before mobiles, iPhones, texting and emailing, once upon a time, before we colonized cyberspace, there was no unstamped or cordless connection with the world outside our windows much more effective than a loud shout. Until only yesterday in the history of human palaver a stationary telephone remained the sole means of immediate communication with anyone out of earshot. I was into my thirties by the time I settled in Britain, where the distinctive double-tolling of local phones took a long time to sound as a summons to my alien ear. Now, the ring-ring called me out of the kitchen of my little terraced house in West London and – ring-ring – I raced upstairs to the bedroom-cum-study, where my only phone was plugged in.

"I have news for you. About your test…" said a woman's voice on the end of the line. My heart skipped a beat. "The results…" She hesitated. "The results…" And then another hesitation. I held my breath. Finally she said: "The results have come back positive."

"Yippee!" I cried out to the empty house. Like me, it had been waiting for a new tenant. "Thank you! Thank you!"

"Oh, I am so glad," said the voice, suddenly young and bright. "I'm so glad you're pleased. I see in your notes you're not married, so I was afraid… well, when a woman's not married the news can be… shall we say, unwelcome?"

Phone warm in my hand, I dialled the number of the next in line for the news.

"Guess what!" I said to him. "Sex works!"

Sex works. And it's a good thing it does too, because – oh my! – does sex not have its work cut out? Whatever experience and expertise we bring with us to bed, no matter how many erotic recipes are served up by carnal gourmets and gourmands, even should the law or an individual's faith forbid specified combinations in the pot, sexual intercourse plain and simple is every bit as imperative as food to our continued existence on earth. And only incidentally to our pleasure. Were it not for the tingles that gather into rapacious lust, nothing in a million years would have inveigled primitive humans into an exercise as ungainly as fucking. Lust drove humankind to first couplings incited – it is a safe guess – by the advancing penis. I imagine that our antediluvian predecessors must have been doing the deed with gusto for a generation or two before they caught on to its culmination in a howling by-product. How long was it before coitus and the need to shelter its offspring brought love into the bargain? Given that every human life descends from a sexual union, it is ironic that differences between the genders are nowhere as pronounced as during the sexual union – and afterwards too, when men arrive fast at snoozing satisfaction while for women the act can continue for nine months before achieving a natural conclusion. And plenty of fundamentalists on this planet still preach that it should.

The contraceptive pill was central to the "sexual revolution" of the late 1960s. Known as *the* pill, the one and only pill – never mind aspirins, multivitamins, LSD or Prozac – it liberated women from nature's little pitfall and soon became the very symbol of our freedom to play with the boys.

When the pill arrived on the scene, there were some vociferous feminists who declared themselves against it. The anti-pill battalion declaimed that if women were given control of contraception – which until then had been stowed in the bloke's back pocket – it would put us on tap everywhere and any time for male pleasure. One small and very noisy bunch of sisters even declared all sex including marital sex to be rape, a generalization that appalled Common Sense and made bastards of us all. What about a woman's judgement? What about her power of self-control? What about her freedom to choose for herself when and with whom she got it on?

Objections of the angry sisterhood to the pill served as little more than a distraction from the difficulty of reconciling exclusively female fecundity with gender equality. The labour of parturition put crippling strain on the "nurture not nature" spine of early-feminist arguments, as indeed it continues to trouble egalitarians to this day.

Revolutionary or not, the contraceptive pill allowed a single woman to indulge lust, her own as well as his, with fearless new impunity, and so it removed intercourse from being the wifely duty it is still purported to be in many societies. Not long after the pill went public, there emerged on the scene a new therapeutic and journalistic specialty: sexperts – women and men with degrees in the outer reaches of psychology who instruct their clients and their readers on erotic minutiae. Thus sexual activity slipped out of the realm of Common Sense and scuttled past romance into a new area of expertise abutting the ancient one of pornography. By the time the mid-'90s rolled in, a proliferation of "sexperts" on the media scene relieved us agony aunts of any further need to be sexually explicit and allowed us to concentrate on more complex and individual hearts and minds.

Seeing recommended sexual strategies become a new section even in genteel publications puts me in mind of my stint as PA to the chef and cookery writer Robert Carrier. Back when I was new in London, before celebrity status overheated the kitchen stove, Bob and I were on a photo shoot to illustrate the recipes in his next book. This was before digital snapping: photography was still a painstaking craft that took its time. Being new to the business, I asked Bob how on earth we were supposed to keep his roasts moist and the drifts of soufflé fluffy under blazing studio lights? By spraying them with hair-lacquer, he replied: a glistening and gluey coat of chemicals would keep the food looking yummy while incidentally making it inedible. Sexperts in print, desperate not to be seen as genteel pornographers and under stress not to repeat themselves over and over again in the limited zone of erotic callisthenics, similarly often try to glaze intercourse with pseudo-scientific glitter.

The pill was less cumbersome and more reliable than the diaphragm of the preceding era: however all forms of contraception available to women still had a string attached:

they could be provided only to documented wives or to girls with "parental consent" – wink, wink. I was around twelve years old when my mother related the so-called "facts of life" to me. Only later, when I was deep into my teens, did she claim her advocacy of "free love", which is how promiscuity used to be known to liberals and "lefties" she admired. Mother herself was a faithful wife who married young and probably a virgin. She never had the chance and never took the chance to practise what she preached. However, it was her idea that even before her daughter had found a lover to fit, she should be fitted "just in case" with a diaphragm at the Margaret Sanger Clinic in Manhattan. Later, during my residence on the Left Bank of the 1960s, Mother used to post me the contraceptive cream to be used with a diaphragm and not available in Paris. In her covering letters she referred to the enclosed tubes as "Aunt Maggie's preserves".

"We won't tell your father about Aunt Maggie…" She wrote of a maternal intimacy that could be seen as more collabora-tive than tender towards a daughter whose name, by the way, was practically an anagram of her own: Myra.

In those days, the newborn in France were named after saints – not a Kevin, not even a Jean-Kevin in the bunch.

Contraceptives were hard to find in Paris, and nowhere publicly available, certainly not to women. When the young Parisian secretary in the office where I was employed as an Anglophone word machine asked me wistfully about American methods of contraception, I told her that condoms in my homeland used to be commonly referred to by their brand name: "Trojans".

"But nowadays everyone calls them 'French letters'..." I said, winning a puzzled frown.

Would she have laughed, I wondered, to learn that nineteenth-century Frenchmen used fish bladders as condoms? It was only a few weeks after our chat about contraceptives that my young colleague scheduled herself an impromptu "holiday" in London, where she booked into a B&B near Paddington Station, one of several in the area frequented by Parisiennes while they wheeled and dealed local abortions that were forbidden in their homeland.

The old witch at the bottom of the lane who was my predecessor in a life of agony used to prescribe a bottle of gin followed by a boiling bath, or the dangerous plunge of a coat hanger, to relieve maidens of their illegitimate burdens, and throughout the 1950s there was hardly any more sophisticated recourse for knocked-up singletons.

Countless swinging young women of the 1960s had to fina-
gle medical terminations with the collusion of sympathetic
doctors. The termination procedure was often followed by
an explosion of grief deeper than reason, leaving a cloud
in memory bound to arise on the horizon later in life. Were
evangelists of the Abortion Reform Act in 1967 chuffed not
long ago to see abortion services advertised on late-night
television? Tragic necessity lifted out of murk into limelight.
At least so it was in Britain.

Not very long ago in the history of sexual mores I still
wrote a column for an American magazine, and in it I replied
to a teenage girl who was in despair about her unwanted
pregnancy. Among the alternatives open to her I included
the name of an agency that could arrange a discreet abortion if she chose to have one. A few days after publication, a
typewritten letter with a Texas postmark arrived on my desk
in London: "We know where you live. We're coming to kill
you!" said the message, written with a twitchy trigger finger
that belied the signatory: "Right to Life".

Our grannies recounted the physical agonies of childbirth
as triumphant old soldiers detail their battle scars. And in
the early days of my life in agony it was not unusual for
young women to confess how much they dreaded the pain of

parturition, a fear that was eased significantly after "birthing classes" came into fashion back in the early 1970s and removed prenatal control from medicos who were trained to treat childbirth as a pathological episode. Fathers-to-be were summoned to the classes, as they still are, to learn techniques of helping partners through labour and delivery. They continue to be urged – even challenged with hints of blackmail – to watch their babies being born.

"What can I do?" asked the daughter of a good friend the other day, patting her blossoming tummy. "He says he's worried about being in at the birth in case he gets sick or faints or something. He says he's not sure he can face it. But it is so important for the dad to be there. What can I say to him? How can I make him do it? He must do it – not for me, for the sake of our baby."

"Hang on a minute. He's going to stay around after the baby's birth, isn't he?" I asked her. "And that's a whole lot longer and a lot more important than being in on the delivery. Please, put away those theories about what a new father should or should not do. Cherish the father of your child for who he is: an honest man who told you the truth about his fears…"

Of course, for a new father to be in on the adventure of birthing and for him to share the first sight on earth of his progeny is not a bad idea. Theoretically. Wisdom never treats a theory as a command: even the most sympathetic theories had better be applied cautiously to the job in hand. The delivery of a baby is a triumph; however, it entails a procedure no more attractive to observe than a tonsillectomy without anaesthetic. Reluctant new fathers coerced into attending the emergence of their progeny have been known to find themselves filled with distaste, even with terror so intense it puts a subsequent chill on their unions. Are we women who struggled so long to be allowed our choices not able to allow choice to others?

"I brought Melissa for you all to see," said the recently delivered mum.

She was a graduate member of the "birthing class" I attended during my pregnancy in 1972. When she lifted the lovely little newcomer up high in her hands for us to see we all laughed with joy to feel the milk bubbling in our breasts.

"Stubborn little darling," cooed the new mum with a kissy-kissy smile for her baby. "You would not come out into the world on your own, would you? My lazy little sweetie, you had to be a Caesarean in the end…"

"Oh dear!" cried our instructress from her platform at the front of the room. "I am so sorry to hear that! Better luck next time…"

In our society – as is still true in many others – fecundity was virtually the only reason a woman was needed or needed to be a woman. Nowadays, worries about parturition and death threats at the mention of abortion are practically gone in my life of agony. However, I was not very long ago told to go to hell by several readers because I referred in print to the "maternal urge", a venerable phrase that is no longer welcome in politically correct if not quite polite or correct society.

"Are you saying women are animals, dumb animals, driven to reproduction like bitches in heat?" snarled an angry feminist who cornered me in a supermarket.

"Nature may be our mother, sweetheart," I replied, "but believe me, a sister she is not…"

To carry new life to fruition is no longer every woman's duty: for the first time in large patches of the world parturition can be a woman's decision. There have ever been sisters in faith, dedicated scientists and artists who sublimate the unmentionable drive to another calling, and there are many other women these days who can see no positive reason whatsoever for becoming mothers. On the contrary, the omnivorous duties of mothering consume time, energy and concentration beyond the nursery and for years after toddling starts. The rejection of motherhood in the cause of worldly ambition can make sense. However, Common Sense comes across the thin edge of many a wedge in a long life of agony, and the alarm bell started tolling between my temples upon reading a recent email.

"Dear Irma, my partner would like to start a family some day. I do not ever want children. I love singing and I want to sing professionally. I'm going to be twenty-three. Have I left it too late to be a rich and famous celebrity?"

"Sing to make beautiful sounds," I replied. "Sing to raise the roof. Sing to find your voice. But sing to become a celebrity? You've got to be kidding! Fame these days lasts as long as the itch of a mosquito bite." Common Sense then added her two cents: "The money made from being a celebrity? It generally turns out to be cash in the pan."

May a desire for celebrity status not emerge as yet another hindrance to a woman's self-discovery and fulfilment – never mind stories every day of another minor talent ruined by notoriety, never mind how many flashy names of the day before yesterday litter the path to the big time. No! No, I am not saying that motherhood is imperative to a woman's fulfilment. Of course not. However, bearing children is a potential commitment that deserves consideration for as long as the possibility lasts, which is longer than ever now that medical research has caught up with Women's Lib, making it feasible to give birth at an age when our foremothers were already foregrannies. "Too late" still pertains, so every woman needs to keep on weighing her reasons not to join the ancient motherhood. Alone among nature's females, each of us is responsible for being as sure as only she can be that before the nursery door slams shut she is on the side of it where she intends to live the rest of her life.

"I still feel sad whenever a pregnancy is announced in my family or at work," said my dear friend, June.

A dedicated teacher in her fifties, June needed an emergency hysterectomy thirty years ago for a condition that would probably not require such an extreme measure now.

"Maybe I would never have had a child. I don't know. Maybe I'd have lived happily without one. But to have no choice, to be a barren woman... barren..." she repeated. "Barren is a wasteland: a waste. Barren..." She said the ugly word again: this time anger bridged her tears.

The off-peak train to the West Country was pulling out of Paddington Station when a breathless young woman rushed into my compartment. A quick appraisal and she seated herself directly opposite me, never mind empty seats everywhere or that the one she chose meant travelling backwards, which is nobody's preference on a train. I recognized the set-up for gossip between female strangers, but with two hours to journey's end, it was too soon to start talking or listening, so I quickly applied myself to the book in front of me, while my unknown companion punched text after text into her mobile phone. Glances up from the page showed me a face that was pretty and self-absorbed under roots three shades darker than their curly length. Nearly a hundred pages along and a baby began to squall at the far end of the carriage. I closed my book; she put up her mobile phone. We allowed our eyes to meet.

"The future is noisy," I said.

"My nephew just turned two, and he could shriek for Britain," she said.

She groped in her handbag for a tissue, not the snapshots that usually accompany references to absent children.

"Do you have kids?" I asked, having checked first that the appropriate finger was beringed.

"My husband wants one." Her voice rose over the distant creak of opening floodgates.

"He's a kind man. He'd make such a great dad. Only I'm scared. I am so scared. I never even knew my father; he left before I was born. I only knew somebody sent us money sometimes. My mother, you see, my mother was neglectful and worse. She was really abusive. She hit me whenever she was drunk. Nobody has had a worse example of mothering than me. I want to give my husband a child. I want to have a child. But I'm scared I don't know how to be a mother. I never learnt the mothering skills."

The train had begun its approach to our station.

"To know an example of rotten mothering the way you do," I said, "it has to mean you know better. You've learnt better the hard way. Who knows better how to avoid repeating a bad example than someone who was stuck with one? Isn't that why we have intelligence? To know better? And to keep on learning better? Maternal love is not a skill, you know, it's an emotion. Maternal love is altruistic: to give is its own reward. And believe me, a wise mum expects no other. You and your child will generate love together, a brand-new love all your own. And yes, there are people who can help you over the past..."

I scribbled the name of a helpline for those abused in childhood set up by fellow sufferers on the mend. No doubt there are helplines for dictating so-called mothering skills; how much more fulfilling would it be for her and for her child to find the way within her healing self...

As scientists and fact-finders storm the territory of prophets and soothsayers, they build their own citadels along the road to eternal life, rational constructs; they are lofty, and some of them very thick. Earthbound strategy and statistics, along with its attendant robot, technology, can enslave us as earlier dogmas did, and nail us to rules that purport to be unbreakable. Common Sense is bullied every day by self-styled clamorous guides who claim to know the way – the one and only way – to be and to go.

"Parents seeking advice about kiddies," says Common Sense, "would be better advised to read *The Wind in the Willows* than how-to books on child-rearing – most of them as dense as instruction manuals for washing machines."

"Your child is not an invention," says Wisdom. "Your child is an ongoing discovery."

In the way of all other urges, the maternal one does not hit all women or hit us with equal force. Nor is the maternal urge the least bit cute: it agitates primeval plumbing set deeper than our brains. The decision to bear a child is life-quaking, matched in length and consequence only by the decision not to.

I was in my mid-thirties when I began to notice the childless women among my acquaintances who were starting to become tetchy, alone in their empty nurseries. One friend, a fashion journalist, tried to appease her quintessentially maternal need to be needed with lap dogs. Another distracted the agitation in her womb with compulsive shopping, a few smothered it under masses of food, and at least one drowned it in booze. My own plumbing had started to roar its late demands for use and purpose, and I had to face the fact that I was one of those women whose soul and balance required her to become somebody's mother. My lover at the time agreed to do his share in conception: marriage was not required, due to mutual bohemian precepts and even more to better judgement.

As my pregnancy progressed, along with a swelling belly grew curiosity. I did not care to know the sex revealed by ultrasound: on the contrary, I preferred to wonder and imagine. I wondered, wondered actively – night and day I wondered who the new one under my ribcage would turn out to be. I wondered what would bring the first smile into a life that was contained within my own and soon to become separate.

"Dear Minus Three Months," I wrote in my prenatal diary, "I feel you sleeping. And I know you are dreaming too. I can feel your dreams flying around and around inside me along with tenses: past, present and future. Before I forget, because

I have started to forget everything but you, I must tell you that a cat lives in the house that awaits you. But I fear he will be jealous or try to sit on your dear face, so I am sending him away to live with friends in the country. Will you frown to know I sent our cat away? Will you think I love you too much? Is it possible to love too much? And if it is, how will I stop myself loving you too much?"

The young woman coming towards me on the London street was dressed for comfort; she wore flat shoes, and a big bag, stuffed and shabby, was swinging on her shoulder. Suddenly, she swerved the pram she was pushing so it blocked my path, and then she stood looking at me quizzically. While she was trying to place me, I peeked under the hood of the pram where her baby was wrapped in blue and sound asleep; upon seeing him, memory zoomed back over decades: I held my newborn son and looked down at him in the crook of my arm; I saw the prenatal dreams depart his eyes as they widened in wonderment at the discovery of sight.

"I feel like I know you," said the new mother. She frowned at a lacuna unfamiliar in her youthful memory.

The baby twitched soon to wake and cry for food. I recollected lifting my baby to feed him, and the moment his breath warmed my breast I felt my ego skip aside for ever from the centre of its world.

"I've seen you on television or something," said the young mum. "You used to be somebody, didn't you?"

"And you too," I replied with a smile, "didn't you use to be somebody?"

"Lovers, careers, power, fame, travel," said Common Sense, "these days women can have it all."

"But not all at the same time," says Wisdom. "And everything a woman chooses to have comes at a price. She must take care not to overcharge herself for something that in the end she can't call her own."

6

Money Makes the World Go Round
(And Doesn't It Go Fast?)

Miss Carnes, Miss Toby, Miss Farrell, Miss Hoyt – and Miss Mabee too – they were all virgins. In spite of their great age, they had to be virgins because virginity was what "Miss" meant when they were teachers in my primary school. My classmates and I had barely mastered the physics of tying our shoelaces, so we were too young to have been instructed in the mysterious "facts of life". We were not too young, however, to know that a "Miss" could not have a baby until a "Mister" asked her to be his "Mrs". He then would buy a house for her to live in with their kids while he went out to work every day except on weekends to feed and keep them.

"My dad says every woman's a miss until she hits it rich," said the tallest boy in the class when the topic of our teachers' marital status arose in the playground.

Future feminists were going to coin the title "Ms" to shield the unwed from jokes of that nature. Not that "Ms" doesn't put singletons in place for jibes too, and smirks of prurient speculation that every woman into her shelf life has observed in response to her request to be recorded as "Ms".

"Ms! Don't you hate the sound of it?" said the young student.

She lives near me in London, and we chat whenever we meet, usually while distributing our rubbish dutifully among the appropriate bins.

"It sounds short for 'miserable'. Why did they come up with it? What earthly reason is there to call all women 'Ms's'?"

One reason was earthly indeed, I explained to her, as utilitarian as it was meant to be egalitarian. In the olden days of forty or so years ago, if "Mrs" preceded a woman's signature on a contract involving money or property it meant that permission would be required from her husband before the deal could go through. And if she signed herself as "Miss", even with evidence of a private income she could be asked for a male co-signer or for her daddy's OK.

One beautiful spring morning, the classroom erupted in "Hooray!" when Miss Farrell surprised us with the news that Mr Guilford, the Principal of our primary school and a man not known for bending rules, had given his consent for her to take us all on a daytrip to the seaside. The outing was

our reward for what Miss Farrell called "good behaviour",
which it seemed to me meant not much more than waiting
to speak until spoken to, keeping yo-yos and comic books
hidden under the desk and raising a hand for permission to
use the pencil-sharpener or the toilet. Good behaviour was
not as hard to pull off at school as it was at home, where rules
about what we could or could not do were also in place and
supplemented by tougher rules about who we should and
should not be.

After an hour on the road accompanied by an impromptu
sing-along, the chauffeur of our hired coach pulled up next
to a beachside café. Its deck had wooden steps down a gentle
slope into a cove. We all scrambled out and ran to look at the
beach below: wide and enclosed in walls of natural granite,
its sand glistened in the sunlight. It was still out of season
and we were in the middle of nowhere special, so even though
the café was open for business, it was empty of other custom-
ers, nor was there a living soul to be seen on the beach, not
even a lifeguard atop the rig. I had been on holidays at the
seaside with my family; I knew that every morning, clear or
cloudy, the sun rose on territory that had never before been
seen by anyone on earth: unexplored sandscapes sculpted
overnight by the tide. Miss Farrell seated herself at a table

on the deck overlooking the new terrain and she motioned for us to gather around her.

"Now listen to me, boys and girls – listen hard. I want everyone to walk slowly down those steps to the beach. And then I want each and every one of you to search for a treasure in the sand. When I say a 'treasure' I mean a wondrous thing, something amazing. No broken glass, nothing sharp, nothing mucky: the treasure has to be something I want to hold in my hand. And do not for one minute forget that I am up here and I will be watching every one of you. Listen, listen hard to what I say: do not go near the water. Are you listening to me? Do not go near the water. And when you hear me blow this" – Miss Farrell pulled a policeman's whistle on a string from inside her silken blouse – "you will come straight back here, where we are now. Bring the treasure you have found with you. Whoever has found the most wondrous and amazing treasure will ride in the front seat next to the driver all the way back to school."

Our hands shot up into the air: did seashells count? What about stones and snails and seaweed – could they be considered wondrous and amazing? Our teacher nodded yes, yes – she shook her head no, no – and finally she waved us off from her surveillance post.

Miss Farrell emerges in experienced recollection as not much older than thirty, tall and slender. A redhead at the start of every school term, her hair grew darker between holidays, and she dressed with what I know now was provocative flair, hinting at contours without revealing them. Miss Farrell taught reading and history with verve; science and arithmetic, however, she sent down from a height of distraction. Our teacher was often elsewhere in her thoughts and always sat apart from her colleagues in the communal lunchroom, turning pages in a book she appeared to be reading. I would bet my bottom dollar now that despite the maidenly moniker Miss Farrell was no virgin: she was a solitary spinster with a red-hot secret. Whereupon the image flies to mind of the principal, Mr Guilford. Memory sees him in his mid-forties: tall and sturdy, he sits in a straight-backed chair behind his desk, another chair facing him awaits the next pupil or teacher summoned for a reprimand. Opposite Mister Guilford's desk at the far end of the room is a fluffy sofa never seen to be occupied. Although there are no photographs anywhere in his office, everyone knows that he is married, because his wife and two stout teenage sons make an appearance at the school's annual Thanksgiving Day party. Mr Guilford is the only male staff member in our primary school, and his deep voice dominates weekly assemblies in the auditorium. Did Miss Farrell hurry us away from the café on the hill so she could be alone with tender thoughts of Mr Guilford, while she sipped a coffee embellished perhaps with a nip of whisky from a flask stowed in her handbag? The fingers on our teacher's right hand were stained yellow, and years later I learnt she died of lung cancer. Whatever were Miss Farrell's preoccupations as she sat there alone above the beach, she was desperate for a smoke, and lit up the moment we were out of sight.

The sand around me was studded with pebbles – silver, grey, white, black, round and faceted, some streaked with gold. No two were alike, and many of them were treasures, amazing and wondrous, but only until surfaces dried and colours retreated into samey stone. As close as I dared to go to the water's edge were the green bubbles it was fun to pop underfoot; curly strands of seaweed were everywhere, some of them coppery-coloured and strung with small shells that my mother told me were mermaid's tresses tugged out by sharks. No doubt Miss Farrell would class them as mucky.

"Look, look, look at this!" my best friend, Judy, was shouting and running towards me on the beach. "Look what I found!"

The white shell she was waving appeared to be no more wondrous than any other on the beach, until Judy turned it in her hand and sunlight activated the kaleidoscope of pastels hidden in its cup.

"Isn't it beautiful? Isn't it a treasure? My mom has a neck-lace that does the same thing," Judy said, tilting the shell this time to make its pinks and blues melt and run. "You wait and see, I'm going to sit next to the driver on the way home. I'm going to be the winner. Just you wait and see!"

She ran off to deliver her amazing, wondrous treasure to Miss Farrell.

I looked up and imagined myself among the noisy silhou-ettes overhead, a seabird flying with my mates, gliding side by side whenever we tired of flapping – can you hear us chortle and sob to see what humans get up to when they do not know that they are being observed from above? The birds flew away together, leaving me to walk alone on the beach. By the time I reached the rock face at its far end, my hands were sandy from treasures picked up and discarded as not wondrous or amazing enough. I turned back towards the water; I looked down. And there it was. There was my treasure. The feather lying in the sand before me was the length of my forearm: it was mottled silver and chocolate, except at its very tip, where

I clapped my hands to see scripted in pure white my initial letter: a capital I. My very own designated treasure was pre-ordained for me. And, better still, best of all, unlike Judy's shell, once home to a tragic submarine creature gobbled or starved out, the bird that gave me my feather had flown away free and happy without it.

Miss Farrell sounded the whistle and started to assemble our treasures on one of the café tables.

"Amazing," she said when Judy showed her the shimmering seashell.

"Why yes, I can see it. You're right: it really is your initial in script," said Miss Farrell, and our teacher was then actually seen to laugh when she held my feather up to the light. "A most unusual treasure," she said, before setting it on the table along with Judy's offering and the pebbles and shells our classmates were bringing back from the beach. A little boy ran up the steps to deck dragging behind him a thick length of rope encrusted with barnacles.

"Maybe," he said breathlessly, handing it over, "maybe it belonged to Christopher Columbus!"

"How will I ever choose which of these wondrous and amazing treasures wins the front seat for the ride home?" Miss Farrell asked.

We made no reply: we all knew the tone of a grown-up's question that wanted none.

"I know! We will put it to a class vote," Miss Farrell said, as if that were not what she intended all along.

"Wait! Wait!" shouted the tallest boy in the class; he was clambering up from the beach and he pushed forward through the crowd of us. "Wait until you see what I found! I found a real treasure!"

"Wow!" said Miss Farrell, and then she uttered an even more unteacherly: "Gee whiz!"

No contest. The tallest boy rode home in the front seat.

To this day the serendipitous feather sits in a vase on my desk. I wonder if the tallest boy in the class cherishes the ten-dollar bill he found crumpled in the sand all those years ago – wondrous and amazing though it was judged to be?

"Please help!" wrote a young woman once. "My closet is full of expensive things I never wear. I have fifty-six pairs of shoes – a lot of them are still in their boxes. Am I a shopaholic? What can I do to stop it?"

"Shopaholics don't shop for what they need – not even for what they want," I reply. "They shop for the person they wish they were. Yet another pair of high-priced shoes lets you imagine sexy thresholds they were made to cross into places where you daydream someone will invite you. And then every time your daydream does not materialize, you submerge your disappointment under yet another daydream induced by yet another pair of shoes. Shopping has become an attempt to control the shape of your life – and of course it is a hopeless attempt. That's how all drug habits begin: each "fix" of the drug is taken to ease the pain and disappointment when the previous "fix" wears off. Shop, shop, shopping for the imaginary woman you wish you were distracts you from the real job, the hard job and the only job worth doing: the job of finding out who you are and who you really can become. A real and wonderful woman is within you, waiting to be heard. Confront her. With her image in your mind, no other, do what you must – a new job, a new place, new friends, a new course of study – to achieve the fulfilment that is not for sale anywhere. And while you're at it, why not de-clutter? Give to friends and charities all the useless garments you have never worn and the expensive junk your busy new self will not need or miss."

"Now just you sit there and be quiet. Mum will be back soon."

The young mother gave her little boy an abacus to play with and settled him on the bench under a big arched window across from the lectern where I stood, moving my lips soundlessly over the pages open before me. I glanced at the little chap and watched his eyes fill with wonder when he lifted them to the vast dome of our solemn precinct. His mother hurried off to join the queue of men and women shuffling forward, heads bowed in attrition, and pausing every few moments at a discrete distance so the first in line could converse privately with the presence behind a grilled aperture in the wall. Finally, I cast my glance heavenward and sighed before scribbling my signature in the little book and then turning to take my place among the hopeful and the penitent. Haste made me careless; the little boy jumped to hear my pen drop in the unearthly silence of our local Barclays Bank.

Grandiose buildings on urban corners that used to be banks are now being converted, most of them into burger parlours. Withdrawals of money concerning us small fry take place at niches set into public walls, where we stand shoulders stooped and heads lowered, communing with our savings, having first tapped in on the keyboard a code so secret that it must be shielded from the sight of strangers, of family, of friends and offspring. Wages no longer arrive as cheques or cash in hand: they are transferred as numbers straight into our bank accounts. Chequebooks are all but out of print, along with the nail-biting sums kept on their stubs. Banknotes are not often folded into wallets these days, nor do coins jingle in pockets. Change changes hands less than plastic does, and every day an increasing number of deposits, withdrawals, purchases and refunds are made at home, online. Thus have pounds and pence gone ethereal to drift along with calories and birthdays, immaterial and unreal until the day of reckoning delivers its sums and demand for atonement. No wonder worried shopaholics have been increasing in my life of agony.

Because it was largely women who consulted the old wise woman, and because women were generally poor in pocket whatever might be the wealth of their masters, her listening ear, her advice, her charms and spells came cheap: no matter how widespread her reputation, she was never going to get rich. There you have one ancient tradition that I maintain. Before high-priced experts and sexperts colonized the hinterlands of Common Sense in print, followed by celebrities who had survived a well-publicized trauma or two that entitled them to claim themselves all-knowing, except for a few years when I worked simultaneously for several international publications it has suited me to be relatively low-paid. At the very start of my public life in agony I promised myself I would not depend upon the unhappiness of others for my income. Let money be the explorer's aim and travels stop at the first vein of gold.

Finance is a language I simply could not learn: it derives from climates where impulse is chilled and intuition is frozen solid. Even if curiosity had drawn me to talk dollars instead of talking sense, females of my generation were never instructed in the rigid grammar of money matters. Women gathered, men hunted. Women shopped, men paid. Women bore babies, men bore their upkeep. My mother was a rare woman of her time, who taught herself to speak and comprehend high finance every bit as well as any Wall Street employee. She saw her fluency as part of a hopeless struggle to control her own destiny. Even after Mother was all but housebound, she continued to spend hours on the phone with her broker holding forth on stocks and bonds while I sat beside the ghost of my father, both of us befuddled by the fiscal jabber.

It was more than a decade ago. I was travelling by Greyhound Bus cross-country to California. Impulsively, I grabbed my bag from the overhead rack so I could get off the bus and have a look at Las Vegas – why not? Strolling around the famous gambling town, its streets registered on my urban radar as relatively safe, even innocent, dedicated as Vegas is to but a single vice – and an indoor vice, at that. After a day of walking and watching, the local ethos finally got to me. I found it not in the streets, not in the neon-lit gambling arcades where every back is turned to everything but chance, while the clatter of coins drowns out words thought as well as spoken: the Vegas dynamic revealed its power to me in the windows of its many pawnshops, where I saw trays of class rings from every major university, engagement rings, gold wedding bands and wristwatches that once were Granddad's. With every new disclosure of foul play in the banking world these days, the image returns to my mind of a silver christening cup in the window of a Vegas brokerage of despair. It was upon seeing it that I understood for the first time how demoralizing – not to say immoral – how uncontrollable and inhuman is an addiction to the flash of a quick win.

We have every reason to be glad in our society that women no longer need to be stuck in brutal unions because they cannot afford to leave their breadwinners. Indeed, the divorce rate began to zoom high when laws were finally in place to allow a wife to escape a cruel or treacherous partner with a cartload of worldly goods and guaranteed support for her and any offspring. Nowadays, after the sweet promises are exchanged and before a date for the wedding has been set, the next step on the road to an altar is likely to be a financial agreement, should either partner have or expect to have finance worth agreeing about. It happens now – although it is still a rare occurrence – that the husband can be the financially dependent spouse and thus the financial winner of a divorce.

"Whichever way alimony is paid, it increases acrimony," says Common Sense.

"Love and money," Wisdom agrees, "will ever be an uncouth combination. A man's heart is not the organ closest to where he stashes his wallet."

A current version of fiscal entrapment concerns adult children who find themselves stuck in the family home without the means to move out on their own. Unlike previous straitened episodes in the feast-or-famine cycles of national economies, this time daughters are among the cash-strapped fledglings as they never were back when girls traditionally remained with their parents until they moved in with a husband.

"I am twenty-two. I had to move back in with my mom and dad when I was made redundant. I simply cannot find another job in the field I am trained for," writes one of countless young women in today's hard spot. "My folks treat me as if they were my keepers. If I stay out after dark, they want to know who I was with. If I lock the door to my room, they want to know why I needed to lock it. My dad threatens to take away my credit cards. I think I am going to explode. What can I do?"

"As long as you live at home, you're a kid: you're their kid. And you will be subject to house rules that were put in place when you first arrived on the premises twenty-two years ago. Do the best you can to keep lines of communication open with your parents in this rough time, share jokes and observations, help out with the day-to-day chores, and don't try to hide your reluctance to impose on them. Whenever your temper starts to twitch, the classic gimmick of counting slowly and silently to ten still works – or you might prefer to repeat the word 'temporary' over and over to yourself until you cool down. Meanwhile, aim to get out asap. And if your eventual escape means working at a job or two that are not what you trained for or ever dreamt of doing? A period of unsuitable employment in a shop, say, or waiting on tables can not only teach you deep lessons these tough days, it will also give you a chance to meet others in your position. Then, you can think about sharing digs till that boat on the horizon finally comes in."

"You might mention," says Common Sense, "that her folks are moaning to all their friends about being stuck with a kid at home."

When I was a child in America, Senator McCarthy was fulminating from on high, and Marxism had become a dangerous espousal. My father stashed *The Communist Manifesto* at the very top of the bookcase, too high for me to reach even after I stood on a chair to make a grab for *Lady Chatterley's Lover* on the shelf under it. My lifelong mistrust of ambition built on the money ladder is not rooted in political bias: it derives from an early attraction to bohemia, where art used to be made for its own divine sake – to hell with price tags or a dealer's commission.

Inherited money was a shameful secret to be kept to oneself in arty circles, where a measure of the artist's dedication was to face hunger and penury fearlessly in aid of creative self-expression. The international crowd of beatniks and proto-hippies I knew on the old Rive Gauche of Paris would never have dreamt that Gerry, an aspiring American poet who hung out in the local cafés, had a platinum pot to pee in. He wore old clothes, he ate at cheap restaurants, he cadged drinks at the bar and appeared to survive the way a poet was supposed to, writing hand to witty mouth. Long after we all went our own ways and I had been living for several years in London, I happened across a newspaper article containing revelations about a shady cult leader in Arizona whose commune had been established thanks to several million dollars donated by... it took my breath away to read Gerry's name.

"What a sucker!" says Common Sense.

"And what is a sucker?" Wisdom asks, then answers: "A sucker is somebody who has something parasites want to suck."

Long before I read F. Scott Fitzgerald, Common Sense had registered that the very rich are not like the rest of us. Except when it suits them to give orders into the ear of the chauffeur, the rich sit in the front seat and find it problematical to trust what the rest of us are getting up to behind their backs. Being weighted with wealth makes it hard to turn and deliver respect or merely attention. All that the rich can give without painful contortions is tax-deductible money – and even that only if guilt or vanity inclines them to give it.

Of course, there has never been a bed of roses free of thorns: the very rich and their heirs fall soul-sick too – and when they do, disinterested compassion is not forthcoming from their community, only medication and treatments to be measured and charged for in cash. So, yes, it is true that money cannot buy happiness, but that doesn't mean poverty guarantees it either, or can be advocated as a way of life except for those few who follow a faith requiring it. Although in the long run the rich may be no more optimistic or cheerful than anyone else, by and large they do live longer and healthier lives than impoverished people do in our cash-based and biased world. But everything comes at a price – even money. And it is up to each of us to decide how many dreams and principles and long-range fulfilments, how much curiosity and space in our open minds we are willing to rent out or sacrifice to cash.

I was raising a child and paying off a mortgage on the terraced house I preferred to call "home" rather than a "first step" on the property ladder, as it was referred to by the agent who sold it to me. My son and I survived by dint of my jobbing pen: word by word, shilling by shilling, hour by hour, often late into the night. Money was tighter than a Victorian corset, laced up most mornings by incoming bills. I had just dropped a piece of copy off at a magazine office in the West End and, having compared notes eye to eye with the editor (for this was before internet submissions), I was racing to catch the bus home so I could greet my ten-year-old upon his return from day school. Trotting down New Bond Street, where every price tag in every window was more than my weekly earnings, I had to stop in my tracks when a black limousine squealed up on the kerb in front of me. The uniformed chauffeur nipped out and raced around to open its back door, and a man who was swathed in robes could disembark and flow across my path. Lowering my eyes from the glare of his passage, I saw a banknote fluttering behind him onto the pavement. And I went for it. Like a hungry eagle, I snatched it. This was back when a tenner kept me and my son fed for a week. I had never before seen a fifty-pound note, let alone held one in my trembling hand. The man who had carelessly let fall my small fortune was engaged in conversation with the doorman outside Sotheby's, and his chauffeur was already revving the limo to depart. The car whizzed away. Grand portals closed behind the Arab. I slipped his cash into my handbag. And then I ran for it. Yes, I was running to catch my bus. But I was also running away from the scene of my crime.

"I'm afraid there's no question about it: to pocket a bank-note when its rightful possessor is in hailing distance makes you a thief," says Wisdom.

"OK. But the guy was a multimillionaire," counters Common Sense. "He never even missed fifty quid, you can bet on that."

"Does that make stealing it less than a crime?" asks Wisdom. "Can one person ever be both judge and defendant?"

Common Sense makes me wonder to this day if fifty pounds, albeit now worth about five hundred, was the price tag on my honour, if not my honesty.

"Stop worrying," says Wisdom. "Why do you think lucre is called filthy? OK, you found a banknote in the gutter. The gutter is where money comes from. And you can be sure the gutter is where it will end up."

7

Body Image Imagined

Back in the fuggy '50s I was a student at Columbia University in Manhattan and Mike was my boy friend. What I mean to say is Mike was a boy who was also a friend: he was not my "boyfriend", nor had anyone else been in the penetrative sense of today's lingo. It was commonplace then for an eighteen-year-old girl to be a virgin, and if I was out of synch with classmates, that was due to my fierce attraction to the idea of living in Europe, specifically in Paris – romantic, bohemian and non-judgemental as I imagined Paris to be. An expatriate in the making, I was preparing myself to reject the well-heeled doctor – possibly he would be a lawyer, but certainly a Jew – who was slated by my times and lineage to turn up within the next five years or so and marry me.

Mike, who was almost two years my senior, happened also to be gay, a condition convenient to our friendship, although it needed to be hidden from the law, from Mike's parents and from all but a group of his fellows in the university.

Fortunately for Mike, male students of his age were not required to live in a dorm on campus as we girls were: he was able to rent a small top-floor studio-apartment downtown, where I often dropped in for coffee and to listen to him hold forth on his favourite poet of the moment. Mike never discussed his local conquests with me: they were his business. The apartment block where he lived was practically next door to Manhattan's women's prison: the big window in his studio looked directly down onto its roof, which was fenced in high nets so inmates could use it as a volleyball court.

It was a weekend afternoon, overcast but dry. While Mike pottered in the little kitchen, I stood at the window watching the women at their supervised sport high above the city streets. The female prisoners puzzled me. Only fictional Greek queens and goddesses had equalled men at murder or robbery or treachery. To be bad, criminally bad, required the perverse expectation of being able to get away with it. Women on both sides of the bars were so far from liberation that it was difficult to imagine how any girl could commit the kind of crime that landed her in jail. Girls were the good guys in those days – unless, of course, we were led astray by a bad man.

"Love…" I said, "it has got to be love gone wrong that put them all there in jail."

Mike handed me a cup of freshly brewed coffee. He looked down to where I was looking.

"Love?" he said, wrinkling his nose. "Self-love, you mean."

"No, I do not. I mean love of a man who let them down. Desperate love, ruined hope…"

"Most of them are just plain crazy," he said. "Watch out, or you'll go crazy too. It's easily done, you know."

A whistle blew, and the women stopped leaping and smacking at the ball. Their shoulders slumped, and a few of them mopped their brows with the sleeves of their uniforms. As they shuffled back to walled-in life, I tried to imagine tales of love betrayed or love mistaken that could put a woman behind bars. What I never imagined – how could I? – what nobody could ever have imagined, was that among the anonymous figures on the prison roof there was one who was destined to become my good friend a decade later in another country. I still wonder if Lorraine might have been the tall white girl who paused and tipped her head back, appearing to return my gaze for a moment before she rejoined the queue being shoved into formation for its return to the cells.

"When all the brooks and soldiers run away," Mike said behind me, quoting from his favourite poet, "time will say nothing but 'I told you so'..."

Lorraine and Douglas, the renegade sailor who was the first love of my life, were both of Scottish origin and grew up as neighbours in an elite barrio of Buenos Aires. After Douglas dumped me in Paris in the 1960s, I inherited Lorraine's friendship and her unspoken sympathy. She was seven years my senior and a dual national of Argentina and Great Britain. She chose to reside in Paris, where she had friends but no kin. Being fluent in three languages, Lorraine soon found employment as a translator for the local branch of a major news agency that was based in New York. Meanwhile, I was working as staff writer for *The US Army Times*, a weekly with its circulation based largely in Germany. My job was to write about everything the wives and womenfolk attached to the American military could do – and, better still, what they could buy when they besieged Paris on their regular outings.

I spent every morning on the hunt for local treats and bargains that I myself could not afford, only describe and promote on an office typewriter. As Lorraine was soon to tell me, her workaday concern was a lot more worrying than mine: she dreaded being sent by her Paris bureau to do a stint at their home office in New York; she knew that when her local boss discovered that her entry had been refused – as it was bound to be by American immigration – because she was an ex-con, he would sack her and then make it difficult for her to find further work as a translator.

We were driving to Lorraine's new flat on the Right Bank; her eyes were fixed on the road ahead. In a tone of affected indifference, she told me for the first time about her criminal past. It all began when she was barely twenty and a declaration of eternal love that she posted to another girl in her school was returned to her parents by the enraged mother of its intended recipient. Whether the girl herself handed the love letter over or her mother intercepted it was not something Lorraine ever discovered.

"Because I didn't want to know," she said with a chuckle.

Fearing a scandal in their small, snooty community, Lorraine's parents shipped their only child to New York to lodge with the family of her father's American business colleague. A generous regular remittance was set up until she found work – or, better still, found a husband. Meanwhile, may she change her ungodly ways and stay out of any more trouble. It was barely six months after Lorraine's arrival in New York when she fell again and hard, this time for a chorus girl she had met in the New York Public Library of all places. The self-educating Broadway high-kicker promised sex and fidelity in exchange for a bracelet she fancied in a Fifth Avenue window.

"I went for it. Went for her – went for the whole damned package," Lorraine said in the tone of blithe nonchalance she applied to her past.

Having grown up in affluence, Lorraine was genuinely surprised when her host in New York was angered to discover that she had forged his wife's signature on a cheque to pay for the bracelet – nor would he believe that she had intended to reimburse him as soon as her monthly allowance arrived. After first securing her parents' agreement that it was time to teach Lorraine a lesson, he turned her in to the police and then allowed the case to go to court, where she was found guilty of the crime of forgery, which carried a sentence of two years, to be served in the women's prison of Manhattan.

"Lorraine, dear, exactly when were you in jail?" I asked, as if I had not already guessed the answer. Yes, I had indeed watched Lorraine at play on the roof of the prison. The image of my friend leaping fit and fast was more than just years and an ocean away from us in Paris.

When Lorraine slammed on the brakes to avoid a jaywalker, Jackpot the First, her sassy highland terrier, let out a yelp of annoyance on being jolted off his perch, and I struggled to sit tight while everything in the car bounced towards the driver's seat, where my friend's massive weight had disabled the springs. Fond memory is overshadowed to this day by Lorraine's silhouette, making it hard to recreate her face or the colour of her eyes. Lorraine's bulk put all else in the shade – all except her voice, so sweet and girlish that a blindfolded listener must think it belonged to a sylph, until they heard her chuckle rumble deep and low.

For Parisiennes of the day, chic meant more than fashion: it encompassed propriety, normality and morality too. Lorraine's size made her a freakish novelty on local streets as it would not nowadays in any western city, including Paris. When she and I were out together, I scowled back at the mocking locals, while my friend pretended not to notice them. I never said one word to Lorraine about her obesity, for she herself never mentioned it and, until she did, meddling superiority would be implicit should any skinny other raise it as a topic. On the few occasions I visited Lorraine's flat, I found her fridge sparsely stocked, the kitchen cupboards virtually bare – even her rubbish bin all but empty. Nor in the cafés where we sat together watching Parisians pass did I ever see my friend nibble calories extraneous to survival. Sometimes on paydays Lorraine and I treated ourselves to dinner at a Left Bank restaurant called Le Cirque – "The Circus". She always left the pile of fries untouched on her plate to be collected in due course by the boss, an old Parisian who feigned concern over her lack of appetite: were the fries overcooked? Was the bread too crusty for her taste? Was she really sure she wanted no dessert? He always seated us at the same table across from the entrance – "your table", he called it. Lorraine did not seem to notice – or she did not care – that "our table" was directly beneath a big framed poster of a circus fat lady.

I sat tight in the tilting car while Lorraine recounted her recent flirtation with a Parisian art student. The young woman made tender overtures, Lorraine said, and she accepted them in return, until one morning she bolted, leaving Lorraine a note to say she was off to join a convent.

"The silly cow is going to live under a vow of silence. Why didn't she keep her trap shut in the first place?"

Lorraine's laugh roared with the car's engine as we pulled to a halt in front of her new address. She was moving flats because her neighbours had begun to complain about

Jackpot's barking. The pooch accompanied Lorraine everywhere: the boss of Le Cirque bribed him with a bone to stay under the table. He was even permitted to curl up in a basket beside her desk and keep a blinking eye on her in the office. Strictly speaking, Lorraine was not her dog's mistress: Jackpot was in charge. Now he jumped out of the car and tugged imperiously at his lead, pulling her girth behind him into the block of flats where the new concierge was waiting to receive them. Meanwhile, I was under orders to stay put and deny knowing one word of French should anyone complain about the car being in a no-parking zone.

Sitting still has never been one of my accomplishments. Lorraine was barely out of sight when I began unloading her packing cases from the back seat of the car onto the pavement. When that was done, I took the keys from the ignition so I could unlock the boot and unpack that for her too. I raised the door on the boot: its handle was sticky to my touch, and a rustling in the sudden draught was followed by a reek so strong it carried with it a horrid taste of greasy bacon and sour milk. All senses juddering, I staggered back. It required a few deep breaths before I dared survey the mounds of sweet wrappers, stained paper, rumpled napkins, empty Coke bottles, rinds, cores, crusts, skins and peels – evidence of solitary addiction that lay mouldering before my eyes. Suddenly, in that Parisian Street, I was beside myself: I became a ruined child – I was Lorraine, rejected and helpless, condemned by my parents for being as they were not, for being the only way I could be. And if Mummy and Daddy could not love me as I was, then who could? Who ever would? Before I could slam the door of the car boot down on Lorraine's guilt and her sorrow, a ravenous hunger gripped me: I was starving – I was being starved for love. During those lifelong seconds, my friend's agony had been mine.

"Addiction is a misery-go-round," says Common Sense, "but no gold ring for another ride: only constant topping-up to keep the cursed thing spinning."

"And so," says Wisdom, "does a drug become the very pain you take it for."

Before eating disorders were included among the newsworthy psychological and social phenomena, morbid obesity was not often seen, and when it turned up it was dismissed as the result of brutish gluttony. Gluttons grew fat: that's all there was to it. Among innumerable classmates of my years in America, the single chronic problem pertaining to diet that I can recollect arose when I shared a flat in New York with three other girls. One of them – the daughter of a pair of shrinks as it happened – used to chew and savour each mouthful of food and then, instead of swallowing the pulp, she spat it into a paper bag toted with her to table.

"A working diet," she called it.

As far as putting the rest of us off food, it worked like a charm.

Obesity has settled into our communities. Couples side by side are seen everywhere to span the width of pavements, nor is it always the woman outweighing her partner – who is sometimes of a size so unwieldy it requires only a dollop of prurience to surmise that "I'm too tired to do it, darling" could be replaced by "I can't find where I put it". Even the boulevards of Paris are paraded these days by hefty locals who are no longer dismissible as Yankee tourists the way the overweight used to be. "*Le patron mange ici*" – the boss eats here – was the handwritten sign taped up on the windows of Left Bank bistros, many of them (including Le Cirque) replaced, as I was sad to see on a recent trans-Channel outing, by branches of junk-food chains. Calorie counts are printed nowadays on packaged food in French supermarkets too, threatening with childish arithmetic the genius of a celebrated cuisine. The way we eat has abandoned hunger, tradition and a little of what we fancy: it is under orders, and thus food has become another way to disobey, to cheat, to attempt to assuage pain and, most of all, to justify guilt. Weight and shape have put other issues in the shade: fat is "bad", thin is "good" – and for those who seek morality in a mirror, it is never good enough.

"Dear Irma, I eat very little, but my body image is still too fat. Am I anorexic? My periods haven't stopped, and I read somewhere that was a symptom of anorexia. Should I worry?..."

"Why ask me if you should worry? You are worried, aren't you? What you must try to understand are neither the symptoms of anorexia nor the image of your body. Understand instead what you need, what you want to mean to yourself and what it is you truly hunger for... "

It would be a fine thing to come up with a single cause of a widespread problem, including the problem of spreading too wide, for then it would require but a single solution to ease all sufferers. But there is never precisely the same cause for what appears to be the same agony – certainly not when it comes to food abuse – so there can be no panacea. Dieting restrains only the symptoms of a central issue that remains hidden and uncontrolled, so it is that weight loss resulting from a strictly controlled diet is so often temporary. Food is a quilt we throw over fears, boredom and anger: we overeat to suffocate frustration and shut the mouth of guilt. Obesity has been known to masquerade as a resident in the empty womb.

"I am not pregnant!" snapped a young woman with extended belly when a gentleman offered her his seat on the crowded underground. Was her rage directed at him or at herself?

Size is admired when it comes to homes, cars, diamonds and incomes – not to mention tits and penises. The noble wives of Tonga used to be locked in cages and force-fed so their billows could trumpet the affluence of the lord and master. Could there be women and men among us making a similar announcement: "Look at me, you can see I hunger for nothing"? Is overweight sometimes cultivated, if not consciously, to create a semblance of prosperity during the current economic downturn? Remorseless nibbling can be a distraction from loneliness, a specious attempt to feel oneself feasting in company. And, of course, food is everywhere on tap: belly-filling stations dole out fuel on every high street, distracting passers-by from the uncertainties of looking for work, money, love and friendship. At least another burger is a sure thing. Diet pills, diet books, diet programmes and diet gurus who supply expensive designer straitjackets have become businesses as prolific as fast-food chains. As for elective starving, what is it, if not an act of self-destruction? We starve ourselves in an attempt to suppress misery, to put an end to feeling bad, to end it all, as exemplified by the cynical "size zero" on American sales racks. I have encountered ageing women who cultivate skinniness to mimic youth, and young women copying the silhouette of a celebrity. And how often is disorderly eating – be it too much or too little – a revenge on Mama, the primary feeder?

"Don't you dare leave those peas on your plate," the mum said to her little girl.

She turned to where I sat grabbing a cup of tea in the local café. "Childhood eating disorders are such a problem," she said. "You read about them all the time."

Turning back to her daughter, who had started playing spitball with her vegetables, she scolded: "Eat them! Eat every one of those peas! Do you hear me? Eat your greens, or you will get no ice cream for afters!"

I had to stop Common Sense from asking the stranger if to pit peas against ice cream did not turn them into weapons for her daughter to use some day against Mama or against herself.

"Help me, please. I've tried everything to lose weight – and I do, for a while. But whatever I do, it always comes back. Overweight is ruining my life…"

"Turn your back on the cursed mirror. Concentrate on the person beyond the shallow image that is distracting and distressing you. What do you want, really want, more than a burger and bar of chocolate? What part of you is famished for a fresh idea, a new activity and aspiration? Set free the unique and beautiful woman locked up inside a body image…"

Making the most of the way we look has always been important to the sex classically known as "fair". But these days in our scrutinized, televised, webcammed, quick-snapped world the eyes have it: how women (and men, too) think they look causes more expense and agony for them than ever before. Women on average must spend at least twice as much time and money on their appearance than on, say, travel, education or donations to those who have no choice but starvation. Even now, when women can at last be employer and employed, guides as well as travellers, mothers and colleagues, artists and models – now that women are not just tributaries, but part of the mainstream – our self-value continues to depend obsessively on how we look. And paradoxically too, because how we look is impossible for us to know. As clichés go, "body image" is spot on: we can see ourselves only as images in reflection, right eyes to left, or in snapshots of how we used to look, be it only a digital moment ago. We can seek our image in the reaction of others, who see us straight away as we can never see ourselves. But wherever we look for our body image, what we find will be distorted by the shifting lens of our moods, our hopes and our memories.

Indecision about cosmetic surgery started worming its way not long ago into the agony postbag. Should she have her tits pumped up, her bump reduced or her droop straightened, so she can be happy at last and feel self-assured? Every time I come yet again across someone who wants to have her very self objectified surgically, I must stifle my spontaneous "No way!" and, having finally caught on that statements of Common Sense are taken as moral strictures, I refrain from saying that I myself would not put the knife to any body except to save it or, if so inclined, to murder it. I implore her instead to wait – please wait – and to heed her doubts (she has doubts, or why ask me?) and, most importantly, to learn more about the cosmetic procedure as well as much, much more about who she is and what she wants from life. True, cosmetic surgery applied to scars and malformations can be life-saving – and livelihood-saving too – for ageing movie stars and TV presenters. However, when it is undertaken by a healthy human being with no practical investment in her appearance, it does not guarantee the end of discontent. On the contrary, if unhappiness derives from a source deeper than the skin being blamed for it – and it usually does – then it will be exacerbated when surgical repairs turn out to be ineffective. And what about the ongoing expense? The work of opportunistic knifemen is not impervious to wear and tear and gravity: it must be maintained and may well need to be repeated more than once.

Although prettiness is fleeting, fragile and more high-maintenance than wit and virtue, its power is indisputable. Not long after I gave up being broke and hopeless in Paris to turn up broke and hopeful in London, the chance was offered me to watch prettiness in frontline action. During a chatty encounter in a pub, I accepted a job writing press releases for a PR firm with an office in fabled Fleet Street. When my new boss sent me to write a press release on a Soho establishment owned and managed by one of our few clients, it amused my mischievous co-workers, who were all men to a man, not to correct my assumption that "The Raymond Revuebar" was one of those underground comedy clubs that were springing into local fashion. And it sure did make me laugh when I entered the double doors off an alleyway in central London to find myself the only fully clothed woman in a striptease club. From the shadows at the back of the throbbing auditorium I saw how the wigglers and pole-climbers held in sway an audience of slurping men – one or two of whom ruled the local world. Backstage, later, I saw framed photos of babies, boyfriends (and girlfriends too) on every dressing table, which I took as further evidence of the detachment, close to outright contempt, for the gasping males in their thrall that I heard the professional nudes express in words among themselves. And I confess my own snobbish astonishment to come upon a thumbed copy of Shakespeare's *Sonnets* in the backstage clutter.

"Pretty women are not allowed to be more than eye candy," says Common Sense. "Nobody tries to see beyond the way a glamour puss looks."

"And so," says Wisdom, "we make a scar of beauty."

It was early one grey London morning, and I was setting my kettle on the boil in preparation for satisfying my new preference for tea over coffee, when the phone rang.

"Lorraine spoke of you," said the stranger in French. "She would want you to be there…"

My friend's funeral was held in a crematorium on the outskirts of Paris. A dozen or so women and a few men sat on wooden benches in the big, echoing room. On the raised stage before us a rectangular plinth was surrounded by a black curtain that would soon be drawn back to reveal Lorraine's coffin and to let us watch it slide into the oven backstage. When the audience settled down, a man wearing a dark suit emerged from behind the curtain. He cleared his throat, shook his head and then, instead of the expected eulogy, he announced profound regret that Lorraine's coffin proved too big to fit into the local oven: it would have to be transported the next day to a larger installation in the north of France. Was I the only one who heard dear Lorraine's chuckle rumbling around us while we all shuffled out for an impromptu wake in the café next door? It was there that a stern woman in black motioned me to one side to tell me that the day before the concierge had discovered Lorraine's body tucked up in bed, my friend had taken Jackpot the Second, her inseparable companion, to stay with a friend in the country. Why? Was it because Lorraine sensed the end approaching? Or had she summoned it? The Frenchwoman shook her head, sighed and walked away.

"How apt of the Brits to tell the body's weight in stones," I thought, raising my glass towards the dark Parisian sky.

Dear Lorraine constructed her prison stone by stone and sentenced herself to it for life.

"Time for a coffee break," says Common Sense.

"And have a slice of chocolate cake. Why not?" says Wisdom. "It will not make you fat; not as long as a slice of chocolate cake is all you take it for."

8

Friends with a Feminine Ending

Nobody will ever know how many shipwrecked survivors in our seagoing history lived out their lives on deserted islands, feeding on sand crabs and never bumping into Friday. We do know, however, that it is a rare individual who chooses to live without friends or companions.

To remain friendless by choice in our human community is a symptom of withdrawal. This, in a few, might be contemplative, but usually the withdrawn loners among us are in terror of something they want to keep hidden within themselves, possibly hidden also from themselves. It is never very long before their unhappy isolation is reinforced by the suspicions of their neighbours. To deprive miscreants of familiars and friends is the most punishing element of imprisonment. And a cold shoulder from the majority is part of the injustice delivered by racial prejudice against a minority. We are not solitary by inclination: we are born to mingle and to exchange. Children who are still too young to cross streets alone befriend fluffy toys and create imaginary playmates to share every day's magical happenings.

Loneliness is increasing, concomitant to our growing reliance on disembodied voices that deliver pre-recorded answers, unequipped to cope with an offbeat or personal question. Not only is service being detached from both the server and the served, ethereal chums abound now too: intangible and odourless, they appear and disappear at the tap of a key.

"I have twelve hundred and forty-three friends," a neighbour's teenage daughter told me – which I thought was a worrying number, for there is more than one version of promiscuity – until it dawned on me that by "friends" the kid was referring to online phantoms she could never hug or hand a tissue to wipe away tears. "So why do you think I feel scared of being so much on my own?" she asked.

Yes, I know, I really do, that if Common Sense is to grow up into Wisdom she cannot dig in her heels against progress. And when it comes to scientific advances there is no question that progress improves lives, extends them and saves them too. Progress is forward movement and Common Sense had better go along with it – at least until progress stumbles and starts to roll down a hill. It has to be held in mind too that every step we take in any direction, up or down, alters our view, and sooner or later threatens to make us lose sight of something or someone we love. The advance of workaday technology puts co-workers back to back instead of shoulder to shoulder, it creates affinities screen to screen rather than arm in arm, it censors impulse, edits spontaneity, encourages wishful thinking, and so inflicts a new and two-faced isolation on our gregarious species. Geographical separation of friends and relatives is on the increase too, thanks to speedy travel, and therefore communications within our fragmented families are often stretched to breaking point. Aboard every long-distance flight criss-crossing the sky are parents and grandparents returning from an occasional visits to their distant offspring. And long-distance partnerships are sorely tested by time and space: this makes them especially vulnerable to daydreams and to jealousy. The latter-day witch on her broomstick hears loneliness complained of everywhere and in every generation encountered in her life of agony.

"Dear Irma," writes a girl – and then, as agonized correspondents often do, she begins with her age: "I am sixteen. We moved again four months ago for my father's work. I have nobody to talk to in my new school. I don't know who the other girls in my class are talking about or what they do in their free time.

When I try to say anything, nobody is interested. My parents don't seem to understand why I am upset. They forget the importance of the kind of trust you only get between friends…"

"Making new friends takes a little time," I reply, while Common Sense must smile to recollect how much longer "a little time" is at sixteen than it will ever be again. "Think of yourself as an explorer in undiscovered territory. Who are these new people? What are their interests? What makes them laugh or cry? Be curious, genuinely curious. Ask the girls you meet to tell you the fun things you can do in their hometown. And encourage them to talk about everyone's favourite topic: themselves. Most of all listen – listen hard. Keep any comments to yourself for the time being. Try being your own friend for a little while. Why not entrust impressions and emotions to a journal until you make friends to share them? Stay friendly, stay curious, and new friends will begin to pop up any day now…"

Friendship is an attachment that is positive and platonic too: should sex happen between friends, it becomes an issue. Good friends have a wide range, from best and lifelong to playful and passing. Friendships can be based on not much more than proximity and raised like tents in the desert for shelter in a place that would otherwise be arid and scary.

True and trustworthy friends hang out together for no profit, only for the pleasure of each other's company. The essential characteristic of good friendship is balance, which is not to say that balanced friends must share the same viewpoint, only that their views are compatible. A Labour voter and a Tory can be chums even if argumentative, because they both respect the principles of democracy. But a fascist and a liberal thinker? They are antagonists and always will be. Jolly good friends are usually in the same age group and in compatible areas of study or work, so that neither of them needs to look up or down in order to see the other eye to eye. Friendship has ever been a support and strength among women, a golden coin in our treasury, so it was no surprise to see how it can flip into an ongoing fixture of agony.

After every summer, holiday moans come my way from friends who travelled abroad together only to find their relationships tested to the point of fracture and sometimes beyond it. Flirting with cute Italian waiters and using all the towels in a shared bathroom can be forgiven in time, even become a source of amicable teasing. But when the light of another land reveals characteristics in a friend never noticed at home it is not always a pleasant surprise for her companion.

"Not again!" I thought. And again I thought: "Not again! The self-centred cow!"

The friend beside me was on annual leave from her work in an English publishing company. One night in London we popped into a local pub for one of our occasional chats, and when I mentioned the journey I was planning on local trains around Eastern Europe, she said that was a cool idea. Why didn't she come with me? Really? Sure, I told her. I guess so. Well, maybe, as long as she got herself the necessary visas. Why not?

Now, barely a week into the trip, we sat side by side bound eventually for what was still called Leningrad. In spite of low-lying clouds, my day got off to a brilliant start when I snagged the window seat at last. Every previous morning on the rails my companion found it her imperious prerogative to grab it. The view was finally going to be in front of me instead of glimpsed in shards across the aisle. As we chugged out of the local station, I watched the sullen suburb dwindle and dissolve into ancient landscape. Because my fellow traveller was ignorant of the local language, in which I could say "hello", "goodbye" and "thank you", I nipped off the packed train at our first scheduled stop to fetch coffees from the station café: hers with warm milk and no sugar – unless they had the brown variety. Upon my return to the carriage, hot coffee stung my hand when my fist clenched at the sight of my friend installed yet again in the window seat, so briefly mine.

"The bitch!" I whispered – loud enough for her to hear. "The selfish bloody bitch!"

"What's wrong with you?" she asked as the train pulled away – and then, because she knew perfectly well what was wrong, she added: "I thought I told you that sitting on the aisle makes me queasy?"

"I'm queasy too," I muttered.

OK, fair enough, every working friendship depends upon give-and-take. But why, I asked myself, why did I always end up being the giver? And, let me tell you, to be a giver is no reason for pride. My unstoppable giving was like my ability to say "thank you" – if not much else – in eighteen languages. "Thank you" pre-empts "I'm sorry", and so compulsive giving is yet another form of apology. Why was I apologetic? What was I always apologizing for? For being a rebellious daughter? For being an expatriate American? For being a woman? For being? I needed no passport for the state of apology: I had been born in it.

"There comes a time to damn well stop compulsive apolo-gizing," I told myself on the train to Russia. "There comes a time to damn well control the giving. Damn it! The time has come for me to join the ranks of takers. I'm going to tell her I want the window seat for once!"

I cleared my throat – I took a breath. And whoosh! Before a word could be uttered I was soaring above our landlocked route and bound for Damascus.

"Stop beating yourself already," scolded Wisdom, gliding over my head. "Yes, there comes a time, if you're industrious and keep your eyes open, when Common Sense finally grows up and crosses the border into my province. That's when you stop worrying about everything that's wrong with you and instead you make the best of being only human. OK, you are a giver. Big deal! Nobody's perfect. But you ought to know that the giving will stop – it must stop – because the day comes when a giver runs out of time, or money, or the will to go on giving. On the other hand takers, the poor schnooks, can never stop. Takers never settle for what they have. Takers never have enough. They must go on and on taking and taking. So give. Give of your best and as long as you can," said Wisdom, waving me back to Earth and Common Sense.

"I stand corrected," Common Sense said as I settled into place. "Wisdom has a point. But one important fact has been made clear on this journey. Travel with a friend will always be her holiday. And you are not cut out for holidays. You crave discovery. Discovery requires the window seat. From now on, if you're smart, you will travel alone."

"This coffee is awful," my companion complained.

"Sorry," I said. "I don't know how to say 'warm milk' in Russian."

Unlike marriage, sexual partnerships and family connections, friendships need not turn sour in memory, because they had to end due to new circumstances and changed priorities. Attend a class reunion and the years will peel back to reveal old friends as spry as they used to be. And frisky old enemies too. Special among every woman's cast of friends is a starring role in the script since the human drama began: women want a "best friend" – a confidante and sister by choice trusted above all others. Best friends have been known to stick together for a long time, some of them for a lifetime. And so it must follow that except for a warring sibling or the wife of a married lover, a woman is not likely to have an enemy on earth as vindictive as her one-time best friend gone bad.

"When I got a promotion at work, my best friend stopped wanting to meet up. Before that, we used to speak to each other every day and share everything. Suddenly she started being cold and distant – and, worse, last week she posted a horrible picture of me when I used to be overweight on Facebook. What did I do to lose my best friend like that? It still makes me cry to think about her…"

"You did not lose the friendship," I reply. "She threw it away. Forget it. Forget her. She is not your best friend any longer. She is not your friend at all. She has become an envious cow. Envious cows don't know how to be friends, poor things. So chin up! Get out there and make yourself a better friend…"

To this liberated day nothing – not a promotion at work, not even new motherhood – can upset the balance between women friends as radically as a new man on one side of the see-saw.

"We used to do everything together and talk every single day. Then a few months ago she fell for a guy at her university. Now we almost never meet and I almost never get any answer to my texts and emails. How can I let her know how bad she is acting, and how bad it makes me feel?" a girl tells me, adding plaintively: "I'm still single…"

"Please wait," begins the reply, as it does so often in my life of agony. "Stand back and wait until their relationship settles down into a pattern that leaves time and space for old friends. And remember it's early days: what if her relationship doesn't last? Wait quietly now, and then you can be there for her if she ever needs a comforting and faithful friend. While you're waiting for a new balance to be established in the old friendship, get yourself out there, and get on with your own life…"

Why does it so often happen that as soon as a woman pins herself to a male partner she unpins from old chums? On a pragmatic level, friendships thrive on shared time, so when a woman can no longer call all her time her own she must rearrange priorities, which is bound to entail shoving old favourites to the back burner: giggling phone calls at odd hours, shared disquisitions on emotions, joint shopping expeditions and, of course, communal cruising in the town. And what also needs to be considered is the fearsome laying-down of unedited opinion, which is treated as a duty rather than a privilege between close women friends.

"Do you want my opinion?" asked the friend I was shopping with, and without waiting to find out whether or not I did, she said: "Get the beige dress. That red rag is too flashy for you." She wrinkled her nose at the dress I liked. "You'll never wear the red, I promise you, never. Get the beige… beige suits you…"

Our shopping expedition was a year ago, and to this day I am reminded of the power of sisterly opinions whenever

I see the beige dress – overpriced and ordinary – still in the back of my cupboard and never, not even once, been out for a wearing.

A number of women over the years have admitted to this listening stranger how much they dread their friends' "honest" opinions of a new man, and more than one has admitted doing her best to keep her friends from meeting him. And more than one woman has also confessed how scared she is that one of her friends will try it on with him. Sad to say, her fear is not without precedent.

My house was too small for sit-down dinners. It was the usual buffet and booze-up I was laying on for a bunch of friends. Charles was in attendance for the first time: a handsome divorcee in his late fifties, he was the latest hero in my long romantic history – and one way or the usual other, I had a hunch he was going to be the last.

"Has anybody seen Meg?" I called out to the crowd milling around the kitchen.

My good friend Meg, a single woman of my own age, was a research scientist attached to a local university, but it was her unscholarly gift for mixing a fantastic Bloody Mary I needed then. Where was Meg? Where had she got herself off to? Nobody had seen her for an hour or so. Drying my hands on my apron I started out into the hall, and I was about to call her name when I saw her: my good friend was frowning and biting her lip as she descended the stairs from above. And Charles was behind her. He leant over and I heard him say: "Trust me. I am the soul of discretion. I will never tell her about it…"

He never did. He said not a word about it during the short time that remained of our relationship. Nor in all the subsequent years of our friendship has Meg ever told me what happened between her and Charles. Nor have I told her that I have a pretty good idea of what went on in my upstairs bedroom. Had I been younger, I doubt that Common Sense would have been strong enough to keep her cool and counsel. But years of observation of sisterly behaviour made me endure with sad and unsurprised resignation in silence.

Avant-garde feminists of the '70s purported to scorn fidelity: were we women not entitled to play the game without rules, as men always had? Having already been living a life in agony for some time, I had seen how sisters, including hardline feminists, grow up competing for love from above. Canoodling with a good friend's guy is not as often due to lust or even to drunken bad judgement as to the competitive urge to be judged every bit as desirable as the other and as good if not better in bed.

"I was at a party, and my best friend's boyfriend was there too. She was abroad for her job, so he was on his own. And I had drunk a lot... and somehow we started kissing passionately. He would have gone further, but there was nowhere for us to be alone. Don't you think she should know what happened? She should know she cannot trust him. What's the best way to tell her?..."

"Do not say one word – not one word – until you have studied your own conscience. And even then, even after you manage to persuade yourself you are all right with your motive for telling her, wait longer. And think again. You say she cannot trust her boyfriend. Can she trust you? And, most of all, can you trust yourself? Or is envy lurking in a dark corner of your heart?"

As often as a newly mated woman abandons old friends, it is the unattached who back off from her and hide their envy even from themselves with a profusion of forged excuses for the abandonment. Envy, witless and mindless, has wrecked countless friendships. It is the sisterly vice, a poisonous hangover from our ancient seclusion in home and harem, where we competed for limited favours. Envy starts young:

it has always been an underlying cause of siblings falling out with each other, and it is a source of bullying in the playground.

When Miss Carnes dismissed our class for lunch, she signalled only me to stay put at my desk. Was I in trouble? No, on the contrary, the teacher had good news: my exam results qualified me for "skipping" – which meant that at the end of term I would be allowed to skip from the fourth grade directly into the sixth grade of our American primary school. Miss Carnes said I should be happy and proud. Pride was beyond me. I would have been happy, or happier, if skipping the fifth grade did not mean separation from classmates since kindergarten and from friends, especially my best friend Judy. While I pushed my tray along the counter in the lunchroom and took on board a sandwich, a banana and the usual cardboard container of milk, I tried to make myself happier by thinking that even if we all no longer shared the same classroom nothing could stop us meeting in the playground during our joint free period. We would still giggle and gossip about boys under the big oak tree with our carved initials entwined for ever around its trunk. And of course we would take lunch together in the communal dining room the way we had since our schooling began. Look, there they are now, waiting for me at our table: Ellen, Peggy, Bess, Diana and my best friend Judy. Tray to the forefront, I hurry to join them and to share the news. But I am too late. They have already plucked my promotion off the lunchroom grapevine.

"Go 'way! We don't like you! You can't sit with us any more! Teacher's pet!" Judy shouts at me, and the others join her in a shrieking sing-song: "Teacher's pet! Teacher's pet!"

Guns were not available in American schools back then: a hard-boiled egg whizzes against my forehead. The clatter of the tray falling from my hands turns every head in the big room. And an invisible knife pierces my heart to make a wound that can never heal.

Female friendships have moved away from the garden fence into a wider playing field. Modern women make friends at school, at work, at sport and in their leisure time, including girls' nights on the prowl. But our new freedom to compete in new areas carries the potential to outshine each other in more ways than our great-grannies imagined. Outshining illuminates the path to envy. Men feel envy too – of course they do. Thanks to a history of overt competition, masculine envy tends to be upfront and seek sporting confrontation. An envious man will fight to beat the other at his game, or cheat to beat him, or smack him over the head with a heavy object because "the bastard was asking for it..." Envious women, on the other hand, though they are rational in every other way, invent excuses, no matter how stupid, in their attempt to justify their hatred of the envied one. Hatred is not too strong a word for the stinking effluvium of envy. Envy boils down to an irrational belief that the envied woman did not earn, did not inherit, did not find by lucky chance her enviable asset: she stole it. Otherwise, if she had kept her hands off the prize, it would have fallen to the envious colleague, classmate, sister or – sometimes – friend. So the envied woman is not seen as talented or industrious, not even lucky: she is a thief who deserves to be despised.

"How dare she flaunt those tits? I should have had them," snarls envy from behind its wall of unrighteous indignation. And: "How can she pocket pounds and praise for the job I was in line to get?" And: "The thieving bitch grabbed that gorgeous guy I never met out from under me..." From the basement of illogic, envy works to betray Common Sense. And it wields a double-edged blade that inflicts as much or more agony upon the envious as upon the envied. Those who feel envy or find themselves the object of it are well advised to recognize it for the hired killer it is, and then do all they

can to outwit it or outwait it, and finally put envy for ever
out of their misery.

"What can I do? She used to be my best friend," asks an
agonized girl, "but since I got my new job she is awkward
around me and has trouble even looking me in the eye. I
miss her."

"Friendship is a version of love, so it warrants an attempt
at understanding before you decide it has to end. Give your
friend time to register that success has not gone to your head.
Show her that your new position has not lessened your respect
for her or dimmed the pleasure you take in her company. Envy
is blazing out of her skin. At least you can escape the agony
of it – so if things do not improve or if she becomes overtly
cruel and hurtful, then turn your back and walk away softly.
And if you can, leave the door behind you unlocked…"

When I finally stopped hunting for romance and settled
down in my professional niche, I began to arrive early at
headhunting parties, pay my respects to the hosts and then
slip away fast while guests on the quest were arriving. It was
at a posh publisher's party not long ago that I bumped into
a celebrated feminist whom I had known in the early days
of Women's Lib. Our encounter took place at the street

door. She was on her way in and – need I say? – I was on
my way out.

"Good to see you!" I said. "It's been too long. Let's meet
one of these days for a gossip."

"I never gossip," she snapped, and brushed past me.

Of course I support wholeheartedly the liberation of
women: what woman of spirit does not celebrate release from
antiquated restraints? If I never became a ranking member
of the movement, that is because I am unable to sit for long
in any congregation of made-up minds, no matter how sympathetic their aim. Common Sense and Wisdom cannot be
polemicists: their work is in the shifting territory between
poles. Also, fundamentalism takes victims, and it seemed to
me that hardline feminists threatened – some of them specifically – to throw babies out with bath water. It worried me
then, as it still does, to hear "equal" used to mean "the same".
Hardliners to this day deride the innate virtues of our gender –
intuitive, pacifist, commonsensical and maternal – which they
evidently believe inferior to butch ambition and command. So
it was that "gossip" became an epithet of general contempt
even among women who ought to have known better.

Human beings are programmed to talk, to talk about
everything – why not about each other and ourselves? When

women were still denied access to podium and pulpit and print, the only tabs we could keep were among ourselves, and so there emerged our genius for gossip. Once upon a time the noun "gossip" meant a female chum. Our great-great-great-grannies and aunties developed gossip and sharpened it into a tool for understanding their society, their families and themselves. To this day freewheeling chit-chat is central to women's friendships. Talking freely together without a chairperson, out of earshot of men and children, is a creative activity. We women describe behaviour, discern motives, spot potential trouble, compare notes and predict likely outcomes: we gossip. There are schools of psychotherapy that are not a million miles from gossip, except that psychobabble is rule-bound and can be a lot less analytical than the conclusions about human behaviour that clever women come to among themselves. Gossip is a route to laughter, to sympathy and to action. It advances hopes, measures opinions and works as a democratic forum. True enough, it is also the progenitor of chick-lit and of egregious celebrity culture – and gossip overheard or invented and then spread heartlessly can turn cruelty into a group activity. But even a kitchen fork becomes a dangerous weapon if it is raised and thrust with malice. Does that mean we ought to return to eating with our fingers?

"I am so lonely," a woman in her early twenties tells me. "I have nobody to talk to. I have no brothers or sisters and I can't talk to my parents about how I feel..."

"To be honest, friendship is not a family business," I reply. "Look for friends outside your home. Get into a sport, say, or join a charitable undertaking. Have you thought about enrolling in a foreign-language course? Start something new that interests you and takes you to where you will meet new people who are interested in the same thing. Can there be any better way to make friends than by sharing an activity you enjoy together?"

At the beginning of my existence as a wanderer, I liked to think of my friends as an international family composed of relatives chosen and assembled en route. Before long, Common Sense changed my mind, and I recognized friendship as a different kinship from the familial variety. A family member has no alternative or opposite: we can have no ex-aunts or ex-uncles, no fair-weather blood sisters, no brothers in passing. We can have foster-parents, yes, but not former parents. And a child-bearing pair cannot be in their children's age group or easily join their offspring's interchange with friends, if they even understand what the youngsters are talking about. Children can be disinherited of material goods and deprived of affection and care, but they cannot change their genes or their memories. Families are set in stone, once and for all, leave them or stay, like them or not. Friendships on the other hand are modelled by hand and baked in clay. They are beautiful and they are breakable. Should a friendship break or be lost to time, a new friendship can always be made.

"We don't want to know the sex," said a blossoming woman in a local park when I admired her burgeoning bump. "But I hope it's a girl! Because then we can be each other's best friend."

"I guess that makes sense," says Common Sense.

"No, it does not," Wisdom reprimands. "Even if she could be her daughter's best friend, what would the poor child do for a mother?"

9

Can Men and Women Be "Just" Friends?

At the end of the phone was a man I have seen through several marriages – all of them his. During the heyday of London's sit-down dinner parties, Chris and I bumped into each other at the homes of mutual acquaintances. Should we both be unattached, a condition more frequent on my side, we generally found ourselves seated side by side by the hosts to maintain the required man-woman pattern at genteel tables. Light-hearted conversations between Chris and me generated laughs, but no sexual electricity: we were not tempted to remain together after coffee and cognac. Over the years we stayed in occasional contact by phone to and from the Spanish coast, where he retired with his last spouse and nothing much to do. His recent call caught me with the question on the tip of my tongue: "Can men and women be friends?"

"Well, of course they can," he said. "You and I are friends, aren't we?"

"We're certainly not enemies," I replied. "But you're a bloke, Chris, so tell me, please, how does a bloke define a friend?"

"A friend is someone you can say absolutely anything to…"

"That's fair enough, I guess," I replied. "But what about saying absolutely everything?"

"Anything or everything – what's the difference?" he asked.

"Anything is jokes and chit-chat and the latest news; anything is all the bits bobbing around on the top of your mind. But everything? Some of everything washes ashore battered by emotions and some of it sinks too deep to salvage. Anything is flotsam. Everything is jetsam. Believe me, Chris, you would not like it if I told you everything."

"Look here: friendship between the sexes is not as complicated as all that," he said. "You and I are friends, aren't we? And you know why? It's simple. You and I can be friends because we never had sex." He paused for a thoughtful moment: "Did we?"

Back in the '60s, when I lived in Paris, local residents did not give dinner parties – or, if they did, impoverished young foreigners were not invited. After residing for a while in London, it was a pleasure to find that dinner parties were the done thing and that alien newcomers like me were invited to them, presumably for our novelty value. Until the late 1960s in London, the woman of the house set and served the table or instructed hired help, and the tradition still held that after the meal had been consumed, the woman of the house invited the other women to retire with her to a neighbouring room, leaving the men to port and sport and politics. Even in hippy circles featuring avant-garde "open" relationships, it was the chicks who left to gossip and do the washing-up in the kitchen, while the guys sat around smoking joints and making plans to bring down the government. And those were but privet hedges between genders in society compared to the barrier reef I bumped into a few years later while travelling in Australia. Nowadays, I find the conversation in the youthful households of my son's friends dominated by female exchanges across the table. The food may well have been prepared by the man of the house, and it is frequently dished out by him too, although he still rarely sees to the washing-up or leaves the table to tend to a clamorous sprog.

The "new man" of the '90s already sounds old hat. He was the first local male determined to get in touch with his feelings – or so he claimed when fanciable skirts were in earshot. He did not pull his weight with housework and childcare the way newer men do and damn well better do (and some of them boast about doing in a sardonic tone, to make it clear their masculinity is not the least bit threatened by the peeling of an onion or the changing of a nappy). Boys continue to make matey friends among themselves at school and on the playing field, where they stand together against the opposing team. Our brothers compete in more ways than a tape measure can show: they measure their advances with votes, trophies, medals, bank accounts and various tallies that include notches on the bedpost. Banks, law courts, churches, schools, big businesses and all other public institutions were begun by men as arenas for tactical war games that allow practically no space between triumph and failure. The male is delivered into life possessed of a sex organ that is designed for war games, external and dangling until provoked or tickled into a sword. Meanwhile the female's primary sex organ is tucked away, warm and welcoming, and always open for a quick getaway too. Young Common Sense giggled upon learning in an ancient classroom that the Latin word for scabbard is vagina. Penis and vagina: sword and scabbard – they are made for each other, yes, and they are opposites too. The scabbard waits inviolate to receive its sword back from rushing around in sport and battle, whereupon their sheathing and unsheathing is accompanied by thumps and gasps that sound a lot more fraught than friendly.

"Sex and friendship are like French fries and roast beef," says Common Sense. "They need to be prepared separately before you can serve them up together on a plate."

"And the sexy fries have to be served hot," says Wisdom. "Roast beef takes longer to cook, but it's tasty as long as it lasts, and it can feed a family."

Is it because females are equipped to carry to fulfilment the end result of intercourse – is that why sex has always been and continues to be more mindlessly undertaken by unfettered males? And sooner forgotten by them too, like any other passing entertainment? During my youthful stint in Paris, I rented a room on the top floor of a shabby hotel. It cost the equivalent of one dollar a night. A beautiful young Algerian prostitute, Murielle, kept a room on the ground floor, and she used to be starting work about the time I returned from my own misemployment teaching English by rote in a language school for adults. Murielle and I often bumped into each other in the narrow corridor when she was awaiting a client or seeing one off. It was she who told me in one of our passing conversations that friendship without physical intimacy between a man and woman is said in French to exist "in all simplicity".

"Like something children do," she said, "before they know any better... or worse."

One evening I returned to find Murielle standing in the doorway of her room watching her client depart. Cravatted and black-hatted, he pushed past me and out of the door.

"*Vive la différence!*" I said to Murielle and regretted the words when I saw dark eyes that were born for sunshine cloud with tears.

"*Vive la différence*," she repeated in a trembling voice. Suddenly modest, she gripped her peignoir tight under her chin. "Without the difference, my baby in Algiers would go hungry..."

Women friends are intimates of conscience and soul who tell each other everything, sometimes more than the friendship can bear. But friendship between a man and woman, if it goes beyond acquaintanceship and approaches intimate memories and confessions, will bog down in erotic curiosity before exploding into sex, real or imagined, or chilling down due to rejection on one side. Whether or not cock preceded egg in the great scheme, the potentials and climaxes of intercourse differ radically between the genders. Friendship, in order to exist between a man and a woman, had better precede the sexual rumpus – an ideal I have observed in my life of agony even less often than friendship following sex. Lust and intercourse, especially among the young, is wham-bam impulsive. A friendship, on the other hand, collects itself slowly. Whether a friendship is established before or after sex between a man and woman, it will continue only if both are determined to understand, to trust and to adapt to each other's ways of seeing and being. It is no bad thing if they are both endowed with the celestial gift of forgiveness. A couple who know each other in the biblical sense must be dedicated to the partnership, or at the very least interested in it, if they hope to know each other in friendship too.

"I am eighteen and he is twenty. I am still a virgin, but I knew as soon as I saw him that he was the one. He wants to have sex. Should I do it?" echoes a current version of a question that resounds throughout a life in agony.

"Why not have other kinds of fun together first? Walk together. Talk together. Aim for the start of a friendship before sex. Friendship with an attractive man is a lot harder to pull off than having sex with him, and worth the trouble too. Hold off on sex unless you know that you are willing to have only sex with him and possibly even that not for very long. How about waiting to have sex until you no longer feel the need to ask me or anyone else whether you should?…"

The current notion of friendship with so-called "benefits" between a boy and girl is more beneficial to one than the other, and not for long. Any sexual partnership, no matter how nonchalantly it begins and in spite of sophisticated promises of openness and freedom, soon longs for exclusivity – certainly on the woman's side. Nor do many romantic, competitive men like the idea of their friendly bedmate being friendly in bed with a new guy. Friends on the other hand are happy to let each other keep old friends, share current friends and make new friends together.

"Jamie and I have known each other since primary school. Recently we had casual sex, but we are just friends," writes one of a soaring modern chorus of "just" friends. "So why did it hurt so much I cried all night when I saw him out with a girl and they looked really close?"

"Jamie was 'just' your friend until things changed the way things do – with a bang. Face it! You now want exclusive bed rights to a friend who overnight became your 'boyfriend'. Can you speak to him honestly and hopefully about your feelings the way friends are able to speak to each other? If not, then please, draw back instead and give him the chance to miss you. To feel himself missing you could make Jamie see that you two are something other than 'just' friends. Or maybe not. In which case, let him go. It will hurt, yes, but only until you find better friends. And in due course, you will find a better 'boyfriend'."

Even those of us who do not like the idea of sexual relationships with married men cannot count other women's husbands among our easygoing friends. The most doting husband flickers automatic lecherous surmise upon meeting a new female, even his partner's friends and the wives and girlfriends of his own friends. A single woman invited to marital tables or bridge games will find herself firmly linked to the distaff side, not likely to be left on her own with the male partner of the friendly pair or ever seen out alone with him in public. Should the resident male happen to pick up a phone call from a woman friend who is theoretically mutually his, he will pass her on fast to his female partner: "You two want to talk."

I pose no sexual threat to my women friends' relationships; even so, their male partners are not thereby my friends too. On the contrary, the men have good reason to suspect that their womenfolk recount their foibles to me, and so they are too embarrassed and sometimes too downright hostile to befriend me. For the most part, exes are another group of men and women who keep a mistrustful distance from each other and invent a semblance of friendship only as long as children or a shared workplace requires it.

Now that I no longer parade the road to hope and heartbreak while sending out sexy messages and receiving them, I can count a number of single men among my friends "in all simplicity". And I confess that over the years I have laughed harder with guys than with women and gleaned specialized know-how from them too, not all of it concerning wonky electrical appliances. I have never had sexual relations with any man I call my friend or ever did – and true, most of my men friends have been gay. One of my best-ever friends – incidentally, he was a man – remained at arm's length thanks to an anti-aphrodisiac characteristic that was equally effective, if more unusual, in my experience.

Rob rented a room in the terraced house next to mine in London, and he used to park his Harley-Davidson in our abutting front gardens. During one of our doorstep encounters I told him that I had once upon a time ridden pillion around Spain on my then boyfriend's motorcycle.

"By Spanish law back then a man and woman needed to show evidence that they were married if they wanted a double room in a hotel. So we used to pay for two singles and then sneak through the corridor to sleep together."

"I like the idea of risking jail for love," Rob said.

"Not for love," I corrected him. "For sex."

"That has to mean a shorter sentence," Rob replied.

I laughed, while wishing I had come up with the line first.

"Excuse me," Common Sense butts in now. "You do know that when a woman talks to a man about her sex life she's flirting with him – unless he's her shrink."

"And even then…" chuckles Wisdom.

I found Rob witty, original and attractive too, until he told me – or warned me – about his predilection for S&M. Ages ago, when babies were still delivered by storks, I used to be posted a dirty magazine that was edited by one of my former colleagues on a clean one. At least, her magazine was dirty back then: it would barely be dusty now. Among the first-person articles and readers' letters I found no act referred to, including strangulation, that was too unfriendly to serve as a sexual turn-on for one who was bent that way. The trumped-up punishment Rob doled out for sexual satisfaction required a scenario, a script and a stage set to be a hit. Under the decorative bits, the whips, handcuffs, corsets and suchlike, humiliation emerges as the dynamic of S&M. To ritualize humiliation and turn it into a fetish punishes the recipient, yes, and also the deliverer, for something in the past and detaches them from guilt. The work of the Marquis de Sade suggests to an objective reader that those who get off on delivering punishment are hiding their own humiliating desire to receive punishment for something they did or thought they did – or wish they could do. "Asking for it" and being asked for it in sexual play detaches the giver every bit as much as it does the receiver from a secret and from fear of being found out. Rob's shaven scalp and black-leather gear worked for him as falsies and hair bleach for many a woman – to hide confusion under a solid stereotype.

Once his requisite pass had been rejected, Rob and I were free to meet as friends at my kitchen table, where we discussed the world, its art, its politics, its policies and the vagaries of social behaviour, now and again fuelling our originality with puffs of marijuana. Although Rob claimed little formal education, our conversations were wide-ranging, engaging and often uproarious. Never instigated by mood or confession, they relied on observation. Should our stream of words tend towards autobiography, only then did Rob swerve fast into a public area of thought.

"You could have been a physicist," I said when he had finally made me understand how a magnifying glass can magnify.

"No, I could not," he replied. "Science relies on fact. And it's faith I'm seeking, faith in something within myself."

Rob's employment as a diver on a North Sea rig meant imprisonment below decks for weeks at a time, locked with the other divers into living quarters that had to be kept pressurized in order to obviate long and costly decompression sessions between underwater shifts. With the others' agreement, Rob started to capture the conversations in seclusion on a tape recorder, referring to the results as "conceptual art". Certainly the tapes were my passport into the men's locker room. Sitting at the kitchen table, I eavesdropped on exchanges more boyish than bawdy, usually anecdotal, aiming for laughs and punchlines with a competitive edge attaching to opinions about politics and sport. The men did not often talk about women, and when they did it was generally in tones of amused perplexity: what does she think she's doing? Who does she think she is? What the hell does she mean by that? Because their meals had to be sent into the pressurized chamber through a chute from the galley topside, everything – even roasts and high-baked cakes – emerged flat as a pancake. When tenors and baritones drifted into sentimental longing, it was usually for home cooking. Through windows set in the upper walls of the divers' enclosure, they watched ordinary seamen going about their work – and a poignant sight it was too, for if trouble occurred aboard the rig it would be impossible for the men to be depressurized in time for an escape: they would be goners.

"All we could do is stand there and watch ourselves sink," Rob said. "Not unlike life ashore."

By the time I moved out of the old neighbourhood and headed into central London, Rob was spending hour after hour of his spare time in sexy cyberspace chat rooms and we were drifting amicably apart. I learnt later from a mutual acquaintance that my old friend married a woman encountered online and went to live abroad. I wished them luck. They were going to need it. Of many offbeat appetites, a taste for S&M and its requisite fakery – even if it is shared for a lifetime – must anyway be unlikely to achieve respectful friendship. Thanks to my inability to participate in his sexual sport, I enjoyed a long and entertaining friendship with the guy next door.

It was just the other day when I came across a Filofax from 1974 that fell open in my hand to the page containing the telephone number of a long-time and long-ago best friend. I glanced at the clock: afternoon for me in London was morning for Mike in America. Before allowing my mind time to change, I dialled his number and gasped to hear the familiar, cracked "Hell-o".

"Is that you, Mike? Oh, Mike, it's me... it's Irma... "

"Who are you? Who's Irma? She's nobody to me," he said. And he slammed the phone down.

Mike and I used to stroll together in our local cemetery: we both preferred it to the local park, which seethed with noisy kids and flirty adolescents. It was in the shelter of a towering gravestone that Mike taught me how to French-kiss.

"Don't be a whale," he said, correcting my gulping eagerness. "Be a goldfish."

Toddling Common Sense discouraged us both from going further. After his graduation from our local high school, Mike left the East Coast to attend Chicago University. By the time I entered Columbia University in Manhattan, Mike had transferred there too. We became neighbours again, and our friendship resumed. At one of our early meetings in an Uptown bar, Mike raised his glass and said to me: "I'm queer, you know."

Poet as Mike was by gift and inspiration and brilliantly well read, he did not need to be told that he was not the only traveller on Walt Whitman's road – not by a long shot. But homosexuality was still a despised and dangerous orientation in the United States, so it had to be disclosed cautiously if at all, even among old friends. Mike was finally discovered by an underground circle of students and professors attached to our university, who all chose back then to call themselves "queer".

"It's only one letter away from 'queen'," he crooned in his bone-china cups.

The relationship between straight women and gay men is as long as history. Any enlightened woman has counted gay men among her friends. Non-conformist girls of my generation used to fall in something like love with them, so eager were we to be wanted for more than tits and ovaries and to count for more than sexual conquests. It was fun, too, being allowed into the closet. While most of my classmates spent weekends at parties put on by all-male "fraternities" of the Ivy League, where every girl was sized up if not for marital potential at least for something on the side, we few dropouts joined lively conversations at a local bohemian hangout before tagging along to underground clubs downtown, where we heard the coolest jazz in town while our guy friends danced together before drifting into shadowy corners.

Upon his graduation, Mike won a fellowship for post-graduate study at Cambridge University. I stopped off there on my first trip to Europe and found him established in the local circle of gay blades. They too were outlaws, only more relaxed and mischievous than the New York brotherhood, and their talk was spiced with a twist of Wilde.

By the time I gave up trying to turn myself into a Parisienne and arrived in London, Mike had been installed for several years in a flat near Notting Hill. He wrote poems for small literary reviews and earned his bread with ad copy for a brand of tinned soups. We resumed our ongoing dialogue and our taste for verbal nonsense. Sprawled on the carpet in his living room while Shostakovich strutted around Leningrad overhead, I shoved the ashtray Mike's way and reached for my wineglass.

"All men are queer, you know," Mike said. "Julius Caesar had no trouble persuading his troops to get it on together instead of raping natives. Having sex made them brotherly on the road and it helped ease homesickness. Of course, Caesar was queer too."

Common Sense soon takes account that those who follow a minority appetite, be it vegetarianism or skinny-dipping or a sexual preference, will claim that everyone else, if they dared to be honest, would – not to say "should" – share it. So my question was not without a certain snideness when I asked Mike: "What about Caesar's affair with Cleopatra?"

"Cleopatra," Mike said, "was a fag hag."

One day Mike quit writing ad copy and gave up his London flat so he could care for his ailing mother in a retirement community of the American hinterlands. Mysteriously, he remained there in the lonesome boondocks long after his mother died. As time passed, our high-masted friendship drifted towards the rocks. He replied less frequently to my regular letters and with less warmth. One day a mutual acquaintance told me that Mike had just spent a fortnight in London. And he had not called me. Our friendship was mortally severed from his side. My old friend never told me why and he never will. A gay man is a man too, even if a woman has no scabbard to offer him except her welcoming heart, and that can be a painful transaction.

Wherever homosexuality is considered a sin or a crime or merely a crying shame, there must be men who need women as "beards" to hide their essential desire. No doubt some "beards" (and some of the bearded too) are hopeful of becoming more than "just" friends. Everyone knows publicized gay-straight marriages that involve a woman who is older and probably more celebrated than her homosexual male partner, whose task is to be secretive about his private life while shielding her from predators and from loneliness. One such union between two old friends of mine was notably long, respectful and happy. Sexual rejection being part of the deal, the women friends of gay men can find themselves cast into one of the classic platonic female roles. With Mike and others, when I was young, I stood in for a sister who was treated with high-strung and amused affection – and envied a little too – for being able openly to attract men. These days, a number of gay men provide me with cordial friendship as long as I am braced to understudy their disappointed mothers, a role that induces hissy fits and chills before reconciliation.

"Dear Irma, I recently met a boy I am really attracted to. I am twenty-two; he is three years older. When we were having one of our soul-baring talks, he told me he is gay. I still want to befriend him. I feel that we have a future together. What can I do to make him single me out in some way?"

"But he has already singled you out! He bared his soul when he told you he was gay. Your 'future together' can be a friendship; however, you can only remain friends as long as independence is granted on both sides. So if you cannot get on with your own love life and without any jealousy or frustration watch him getting on with his love life, then friendship between you will not be possible. It would be better to wish him luck and bid him goodbye, at least for the time being. And then to find yourself a guy who bares his soul to you, yes, and wants to bare more..."

To this day our atavistic prejudices militate against friendship between the sexes. Any curious reader of love "want" ads will note the number of women in search of a soulmate who still require him to be taller. What on earth for? So he can reach a higher apple on the tree? Or is it to shield her and their offspring from pterodactyls? Heightism is rampant as well as ageism on both sides. Why must she be younger to please him? Lest observers suspect he is too old to satisfy a lusty girl? And why does she require him to be older? So he will be likelier to predecease her, and thus leave her and the children provided for? Or does she imagine that a judgement more mature than her own will allow her to stop bothering to learn? Even in these relatively liberated times, he'd better be richer than she is if he hopes to win the approval of her family. And so to a problem arising all too often in a life of agony when bigger richer partners fail to control themselves and abuse the power that muscle and money gives them over shorter, poorer helpmeets.

"We have been living together for three years. I love him and he tells me he loves me too," writes a woman, followed by the "but" that can always be expected after an expression of love in a life of agony, "but when he gets angry, he hits me... he's always sorry afterwards. Only, it makes me so worried. What can I do about it?"

"Leave him," I reply, for this is one problem that allows me to be opinionated – to be prejudiced, in fact. "Physical abuse debases love. Repeated abuse, no matter how often the abuser says 'sorry', destroys any hope of long-term friendship. It is up to him: he must discover the true origin of his destructive anger and then learn how to control it. Unless he goes voluntarily for counselling about understanding and controlling his anger, it would be unwise and even dangerous for you to stay within striking distance. I'm sorry, but experience makes me ask you to consider something else too. I must ask if he is your first physically abusive partner. If he is not your first – and if you truly want him to be your last – then you will need to trace the cause in your own history and heal the wound that makes you believe you deserve no partner better than a ham-fisted brute…"

And I attach the appropriate helpline, required and available in a modern life of agony.

Women are once in a great while accused of physically abusing their partners. However, since males are generally the huskier of a pair, they are much, much more often the villains – far too often in my world of agony. A woman can be as enraged as a man, equally out of control as he is and every bit as nasty, but the chances are she does not pack his punch.

"Poison is a woman's traditional weapon," says Common Sense, "so he'd better watch out if she packs his lunch."

"Friends? Men and women? Not in a million years!" exclaimed the chairperson of the local Women's Institute. She had rung to invite me to address their next meeting and caught me in mid-ponder. "Men and women might as well be a different species."

"And if we stopped being different one way or another," I asked, "would our species last another generation?"

"No fear," she replied. "They'll be making babies in test tubes any day now, and we won't need sexual differences after that. Maybe in a thousand years men and women will all be, you know – what do they call them? – hermaphrodites! And then they can be friends at last."

"I hope not!" We roared with laugher into our separate phones.

"To hell with political correctness," she said.

Common Sense chuckles: "Political correctness is codswallop!"

Wisdom agrees: "PC is codswallop. But you'd better learn how to speak it anyway. Coming across as politically correct could save your life some day the way it saved them in Stalin's Russia and Hitler's Germany."

10

Snake-Belly Lows

The railway station at Calais-Fréthun on the French Channel coast must have been designed to be passed through at high speed. There is no news-stand, no duty-free shop; available seating is metallic and, as far as frequent travellers can tell, the café opens and shuts on the whim of its proprietor.

A weekday morning in early December and a small group of us had been stranded for more than two hours in the departure lounge on the far side of immigration. We were awaiting the delayed Eurostar train from Paris to London without even a coffee machine to offer comfort. An English couple were doing their best to entertain a fretful toddler; two Belgian tourists tried to snooze on the unyielding benches; and the French businessman in a dark suit paced back and forth before finally settling down with his portable computer. Minutes gathered and marched towards high noon while I shivered in my quilted coat: no official was in sight for us to ask: "Excuse me, why in mid-winter have you turned off the heating? And please, please, would you please turn it on again?" The third hour was well along by the time an announcement of our train's imminent arrival flashed up on the so-called Information Board and a uniformed attendant materialized out of his cosy employees' lounge to summon us onto the windswept platform.

"A breakdown?" I asked him over the roar of the incoming train.

"No, no breakdown," he said, standing back so the English couple could haul their child and suitcases up into the train. "A young man threw himself on the tracks outside Lille. The driver was too upset to go on. They had to wait for his replacement."

"I call that a breakdown," whispers Common Sense. "How dreadfully out of a repair must a young person be to leap in front of an oncoming train."

"And incidentally," says Wisdom, "make an executioner of its driver."

I walked through the compartment to the window seat I had reserved, only to find that as usual a Parisian boarder had occupied it. The middle-aged Frenchwoman looked up with a frown and then started to gather her books and bags and gloves. The short journey ahead of us passed through a farmed and man-made landscape that I knew by heart, but it could well be foreign and new to her, so I told her to please stay put at the window and, after stashing my bag overhead, I settled into the aisle seat beside her. The air around us bristled with exclamations and exchanges in her native tongue and in my own.

"How could he be so bloody inconsiderate…"

"*Espèce de con…*"

"We're going to miss our connection at Euston Station thanks to that thoughtless…"

"*Il ne pensait pas aux autres…*"

As the train descended into the tunnel connecting those sometime enemies, our two homelands, the Frenchwoman and I exchanged looks of sorrowful perplexity.

"What is it you say in English? Misery like company?"

"Yes," I said. "And so does anger…"

Anger and misery: head and tail of one coin in the bank of emotions. When suicide is committed in youth and good health, anger has its finger on the trigger. What other emotion is fiery enough to ignite a young mind brought low by disappointment or shame or jealousy? "This'll show you!" Trite though it might sound, this can prompt self-immolation, while hurling at the same time a challenge at individual survivors and at society in general: why did we not care better or enough? Had we cared more, could we not have prevented the victim's terminal decision? I wish had not needed to ask myself this unhappy question or ask it more than once.

Cora was one of only a few black girls who were resident in the dormitory of my college. Her room was next to mine, and she popped in from time to time to chat and compare notes.

"I always feel like I'm walking into the Minetta Tavern," she said with a nod at my empty beer keg: I had come across it outside a bar on Broadway and rolled it forty blocks uptown to serve a new purpose as my bedside table. Cora and I exchanged a smile – not many girls at my posh college knew about the Minetta Tavern, an arty hangout in the West Village that was still the bohemian centre of Manhattan back in the '50s.

"And you even have a resident poet," Cora said, nodding this time towards the volume of John Donne's poems atop the beer keg.

At one of our early meetings Cora mentioned that her father was the president of a college in the deep South, the first ever to be established for descendants of the enslaved.

"And I'm his only child," she said – then added a sardonic: "Who's a lucky girl?"

Cora was not academic by nature. She must have been strenuously coached to pass our stiff entrance exam, and of course I wondered why her father wanted her to attend a bluestocking Northern women's college instead of his own school. But she saw the question coming before I could ask it. She shifted her eyes away from mine and changed the subject fast to a problem with her paper on *The Canterbury Tales*.

Cora had a passion for classical music, as well as the great jazz of the day. It was a joy to hear her ripe voice singing through the thin wall between our rooms, so when she did not return after summer break I assumed she must have switched to a school up her musical street. It was several weeks into the new term before I learnt that Cora had hanged herself.

"Rather than disappoint her father by flunking out," is how her tragedy was explained by the campus gossip who told me.

I nodded sorrowfully, not in agreement. I was nodding in time to a ditty from childhood that clanged between my ears: "Nobody loves me, everybody hates me. I'm going to go and eat worms."

Should just the hint of suicide arise in my life of agony I urge the suffering person to counselling and self-help groups that have been set in place at last in our society to aid the depressed and help lift heavy hearts. It is true that not everyone who considers suicide or all who threaten it aloud will commit the dreadful deed. However, there is a stubborn and defensive old misconception still at large that anyone who speaks to another or others about suicide never actually does it. In fact, suicide is premeditated murder: people who kill themselves have thought about how they intend to do it, and they have probably spoken of it too. Call it a cry for help. Thus guilt must corrupt the grief of survivors to punish even those who were not near enough or barely dear enough to have prevented the deed.

It was early night in London. I had tucked my son into bed and was settling down in front of the telly when a sharp knock came at my front door. The sight of a uniformed policeman on the threshold filled me with innocent alarm. He was there to tell me, gently and hesitantly, that my occasional childminder, Eric, had killed himself. And in the note written before putting his head in the gas oven, Eric gave my name and address as one to notify.

"But what about his parents?…"

"His parents were notified of course, in the normal course of things."

"The normal course of things…" I repeated the policeman's words, and again as a question: "The normal course of things?"

"He was just a kid," the policeman said, his brow wrinkled over thoughts of his own child or children. "He had his whole life ahead of him."

"In the normal course of things," the policeman and I repeated sorrowfully in unison.

Not long before Eric's death, he and I were sitting alone together in the sunny back garden while my young son took an afternoon nap upstairs. It was then that Eric told me his parents could not accept his homosexuality as being in "the normal course of things".

"They want me to go for a cure. Some quack has told them about a place where I can go and get treated. Can you believe it? Treated for what? For being me? As if they gave a damn who I am. As if they cared! As if they'll care if I do myself in…"

Eric was sitting on my son's swing, and the kick he gave the ground beneath his feet all but sent him backwards over the frame. It was only a week after our chat in the garden when the policeman delivered the bad news that caused me countless sleepless nights of wondering: "What could I have done to save Eric's life? What should I have done? Should I have believed him instead of assuming overstatement? Should I have said more than: 'Eric, dear boy, give them time to change. Give yourself time too, and a chance to organize your independence. And most of all, Eric dear, give life a chance to get better'?"

It did not help in the aftermath of Eric's brief life to know that the burden of survivor's guilt his parents inherited must be lifelong and infinitely heavier than mine.

"Hello, how are you?" asked a friend not long after the Christmas festivities.

"I'd have to look up to see a snake's belly," I replied. "What about you?"

"I'm feeling low too. They said on the radio that today is the lowest day on the calendar."

"Really? Since when?"

"Isn't it always since records began?"

Depression can be brief or can be chronic. It can range from passing episodes to mind-threatening infection. The doldrums are contagious among friends and family members, as well as being infectious within the community. Before Seasonal Affective Disorder – SAD – was assigned a pompous moniker to take its place among pathological disorders requiring support groups, pills, sun lamps and pricey treatments, it used to be known as "dark-day blues" or "black-dog lows". When sufferers announce chronic seasonal lows to me, if a restorative trip to the sunshine is beyond their means or convenience, I recommend they seek local distractions to help them through the clouds. When my own days go SADly, long walks – even if they must be under an umbrella – help to deprive depression of the physical energy it devours for survival. Sometimes I invite myself to a cinema, where I scoff a box of popcorn while my mind flies over the storm to make-believe. Athletic friends head for tennis courts, swimming pools, golf courses and exercise gyms.

Seasonal blues are not the only form of low spirits that descend on communities at large. Ever since instantaneous reportage gave all nations neighbouring doorsteps, a war being waged anywhere on the globe, a civilian massacre or the disgrace of an internationally respected figure can send gloomy tremors throughout universal equanimity. And what about the daily moans of depressed economy, MAD

– Monetary Affective Disorder? MAD claimed lives back in the 1930s and is threatening them again.

Influences on an individual's depression can vary according to his or her society, and easing the dark moods depends upon what kind of help is at hand. For a few prosperous years in the late '70s, I was employed to write agony columns in an American publication as well as one in South Africa and another in Japan. South Africa was still burdened by Apartheid. As the letters arriving on my desk revealed no colour other than the ink in which they were written, I dared not suggest that my correspondent move away from the source of her pain, say, or find a new job, change schools or consult the authorities, lest racist laws forbade it. Japanese women wrote to me infrequently about romantic lows; more often they were brought down by gloom induced by employment, by families and in-laws, especially mothers-in-law. Visits to that beautiful island nation revealed a gender divide that was accepted and still maintained pretty much as depicted in the eleventh-century *Tale of Genji*. Men were seen in the evening reading newspapers in the front seats of their parked cars, wheeled islets of peace and quiet in frenzied Tokyo, where a few domestic walls were still made of paper. And should a Japanese supplicant write a dark message induced by shame, guilt or betrayal, I worried and wondered if the translator between her and me had edited out any reference to suicide in a society where self-immolation has always held a place of honour. As for agony in my former homeland, where "the pursuit of happiness" is a constitutional guarantee that was essential in its time to Suffragettes and other avant-garde movements, the right to "pursue" happiness was regularly misconstrued by those who wrote to me as the right to have it. American agony post blazed with angry blame of specific others for depriving the correspondent of what she evidently took to be her entitlement.

It was the early '70s. An American wrote in rapid angular script how much she had wanted to kill her cheating ex before he left her. Instead, she opened the glove compartment of her car, grabbed her gun – which was not at all an unusual accessory for women in her part of the world – and shot dead the hitch-hiker she had picked up on a country road. She then shoved his corpse out of her car and zoomed away. Her problem was that the deed had started to weigh heavy on her conscience and make her suffer bouts of darkest depression.

"I will never be able to have a normal life. I don't know what to do."

A smudged postmark on the envelope showed only the date and the State it was sent from, but there was no name, no address, not even a signature, only the word: "Wretched". What could I do, except hope that writing to me was Wretched's first step towards repentance? Capital punishment was in effect in her state of the Union, so I had to hope too that she would seek private therapy or, if applicable, make a confession to her priest – anything other than surrender herself to homicidal legislation. And yes, it was a genuine letter. How do I know? Because the words rang true. It does not take long in a life of agony to recognize the hollow tone of a fake letter, often written by men who are pretending to be women, many of them describing in detail what they purport to be wearing before stating their imaginary problems.

"What if…" In the chill of a lonesome Parisian evening, I leant over the railing of the bridge and half-spoke, half-thought: "What if…"

It was my thirtieth birthday, and as far as I could tell the day had passed unmarked by any other living soul. Even in these long-lived times, for a solitary or undecided woman the thirtieth year pops up as a signpost on the road to failure and depression. Flat-broke after nearly a decade abroad, ever

IRMA KURTZ

rootless and looked upon with disdain (or so I interpreted the disinterest of my Parisian neighbours), dragging shattered love affairs and employed in a job that lacked challenge or potential, I saw nothing more of my youthful dream, nothing left for me to do except go back to a homeland I had abandoned, back to the lash of "we told you so" and back to disappointment without reprieve. And what was disappointment if not the appointment with fulfilment that I had failed to keep? There was nothing in front of me, only the rolling Seine. So what if I hoisted myself up and over and into the river? So what if I ended for ever there in Paris where countless American-born dreamers had ended their dreams long before mine had begun? Was I angry at Paris? No. Paris was what she turned out to be: a formal garden, elegant and walled-in. Was I angry at my parents for failing to support me in my adventurous undertaking? How could I be angry at them? They did what they believed to be for the best. Was I angry at myself? No, not even that. I could rouse no anger at all: I was too tired to be angry, exhausted beyond my years and my experience. Only the Seine glittered with possibility of something to do – one final act I could commit without help or a command. Suddenly a gust of wind tore the kerchief from my hair and flew it spinning out of my reach, until it dropped into the river below, where I saw it floating as I would not float. And then, as the silken scrap twisted down into choppy water, a memory drifted back to me.

I was holding my father's hand at the height of my shoulder while we strolled together under red maple trees. My father stopped and pointed to the path at our feet: there lay a silver bird, eyes unseeing, its wings broken and flightless.

"The bird is dead," my father said.

"Dead…" I said the word for the first time.

"Dead means it's all done. Finished. Kaput," my father said.

"So the little bird will never know what happens…" I thought.

All those years later on the Pont des Arts I thought: "To jump off this bridge means never to know what happens."

Depression quivered, hovering. Life-loving curiosity triumphed. A lonely end was not all that remained of my future – not yet. I was going to cross the bridge. I wanted to find out what happens. It was to be only a few days before I sold up my Parisian flyspeck and crossed the Channel to London, where every day has been more interesting and more fun than throwing myself off the Pont des Arts.

"You see," says Wisdom now, "you learnt then that happiness is not the aim of setting out into the world: happiness can be but a by-product of the journey."

Inertia, a dull pointlessness that defies heartbeat, is one indication of deepest depression. I was barely six years old the first time my father took to his bed in retreat from mother and me, from my baby brother, from work, from music, from sunshine and from life itself. The aroma of oranges arises now in memory out of the glass Mother gives me with instructions to take it in to Daddy and please, Irma, please try to make him smile. Two single beds are side by side in my parent's room. My father lies on the one nearest to the window and his back is turned to the open doorway, where I stand with my mother watching anxiously from behind me.

"Daddy, please, please…"

When my father turns my way at last, I watch his heavy eyes struggle and finally focus to see me holding up the glass of orange juice. A smile twitches hopelessly around his mouth, which remains downturned like the entrance to a tunnel. He groans and shakes his head, and his dark gaze leaves me to turn back to the clouds outside his window. Many years later Mother told me that after another of several similar episodes my father was subjected to electroconvulsive therapy, which was still routinely prescribed in those days for chronic depression and only abandoned later as burning and destructive: a functioning analogy for anger.

Hurt feelings are inwardly turned, isolating and self-absorbed. They express themselves in self-blame and self-effacement. Whenever I suffer from the hurt feelings that attack apologetic natures, I try consciously to make myself angry, just a little angry – angry at something or at someone other than myself. Anger has a bad name, and has earned it too, for in its extreme state it leads to vengeance and destruction and, blinded by wildfire, it can take innocent victims. However, anger is an emotion that generates outward energy as hurt feeling cannot do. Therefore, small and controlled doses of anger can help spur a struggle out of depression and its attendant inertia. And in due course, when depression and self-blame have finally subsided, anger – even if it is righteous – cools down enough to be pushed aside in favour of objective understanding.

The woman was tired. Blue shadows under her eyes made them look too old for her years, which were not many over thirty. She and I were waiting in our doctor's surgery. I was there for an annual flu jab, and she in hope of a more esoteric treatment.

"I'm so depressed," she said to me, as to an old friend. "After three years together, he dropped me last month for someone else. I'm so depressed I don't even want to get up in the morning. I can barely manage to drag myself into work. I keep reading all the old letters and emails, where he said he loved me. And we had made holiday plans. And then he leaves me, without a word – off he goes with someone he must have been seeing on the side. Who knows for how long? I feel worthless, used. I'm scared even to leave my flat" – she cast a dark look at the door to the street – "in case I meet someone who asks about him. Or what if I bump into him?"

"Those love letters," I said, surprised by my rush of anger on her behalf, "they stink. Old rubbish always stinks. Why don't you scrap them? And delete the emails. Why not?" I paused for a moment to calm down. "Or give them to someone you trust," I said, hoping silently that she had a trustworthy friend or family member in her life, "who will hold them until you feel ready to face them without tears. You could do the classic thing too. I've read about it. I mean you could shred any clothes or stuff he left behind and bin it. Then invite a few good friends over to lift a glass. So what if they ask about him? Tell them you've finished with the useless son of a bitch. Or at least say 'thank Heavens!'" I added quickly, in case the flash in her eye was not incipient anger, only disapproval of bad language. "Sound angry, is what I'm trying to say. It can help you feel angry. Be angry. You're entitled to be angry. The guy is a useless…" I settled for: "…rat. And if you bump into him? Give him the cold shoulder and walk on by. He asked for it, the double-crossing cheat. If you let it, the day will come when you thank your lucky stars the self-centred piece of… ordure… left you free to enjoy your better new life."

"He is a con man," she said, and I detected a pinch of anger that became more evident when she repeated the words in the past tense: "He was a con man… the son of a bitch!"

I hoped a dose of justifiable anger might obviate her desire for the anti-depressants she was there to request.

"Here is an injustice to consider," says Wisdom. "Why is self-pity the only version of compassion held in universal contempt?"

When depressed people have a specific reason for misery – a broken relationship, a broken leg, a broken promise or lost employment – to ask them: "Why are you depressed?" is redundant: they have already told their friends, sympathetic family members and workmates what ails them, nor will they hesitate to tell everyone again, not until logical depression finds a logical solution and resolves itself. However, when depression is chronic and amorphous, when it is related to displacement of values, to loss of self-worth, to guilt, to abject loneliness or to a mortal fear beyond telling or facing, then to ask why they are depressed must exacerbate their pain, because it can elicit only "I don't know" as an answer.

Profoundly unhappy people can hesitate to confide their condition precisely because they dread being slapped with a less than useless: why? Depressed men and women deserve uninterrupted listening to, even their silences heard without comment, until they themselves are ready to hear what they themselves have to say. Fortunately, local counsellors and self-help groups exist at last; their brochures are available in every health centre.

The two young women chanced to be my neighbours in a Soho coffee shop.

"I cannot stop doing it," the pale thin one said to the bouncing girl of about her own age. "I've tried. I just cannot stop."

She rolled up her sleeve to show her companion – and incidentally me too – the scars, a few of them still red and raw, criss-crossing her inner arm. Whereupon the skinny girl turned suddenly to look straight at me, and I watched the small notoriety attached to my life in agony dawn in her eyes.

Dutifully, I asked her: "Counselling?"

"I tried it," she said. "But the counsellor wouldn't listen. She kept interrupting."

"Well, counsellors aren't judges. No counsellor can be the right one for every applicant. Human chemistry is involved too: when is it not in our one-on-one contacts? And there are counsellors who can't lift themselves higher than theories they've learnt and need to keep proving. But the counsellor for you is always out there: someone who will listen to you and let you listen to yourself too, not just to him or her. Your counsellor will help you to a solution, even one that might not work for someone else in the same spot. Please, don't give up. Promise – and I mean promise yourself – to shop around for the help that helps you..."

I asked the scarred girl for her email address so I could send her a list of specialists in self-harm.

"But couldn't you do it? Aren't you a counsellor?"

"Me? No. I'm no counsellor. I'm just an old busybody."

She laughed, which is always a good start towards recovery.

Yet another gender discrepancy must be added to the collection. Pre-menstrual, post-natal, and menopausal: these natural episodes of depression are inflicted on women literally like clockwork. Men don't get them. Women who live together in a university dormitory, say, in barracks, in prison or on shipboard, and no doubt women in harems too, find that their menstrual cycles become mysteriously coordinated along with attendant downers. And as uterine synchronicity means that the cohabitating wives of one husband ovulate more or less around the same time too, there is a good chance they will fall pregnant in unison, all inseminated by their mutual supplier.

Nature's pragmatic genius defies wishful thinking, her secrets open only to science – and some of them to Common Sense. Common Sense suggests that sororal timekeeping emerged out of nature as a life-saving device. Women who fell pregnant simultaneously would therefore lactate simultaneously too, and so they would be able to feed each other's babies should new mothers be lost as so many were in ancient childbirth. Meanwhile, grannies make menopause downright beneficial by being available to keep the tribe's toddlers safe and fed while younger women are occupied with bearing and feeding the newborn. And thus when women are sequestered can sisterly bouts of depression rule the roost, incidentally subduing any unruly urge among procreating females to go out and have some fun. Of course, a woman's freedom at last from the rules of the harem cannot end her depressions; only move them to a bigger world she shares with brothers as well as sisters.

"Depression is wrecking my relationship and it's ruining my life," a woman writes. "I hate the way I feel… do you think I need anti-depressants?"

"Depression is a painful condition. Sometimes an episode of depression is so dangerously agonizing that it merits prescribed chemical ease. But painkillers are a lot easier to start than to stop. So before you start taking pills, please consider the pain of your depression not as an illness, but as a symptom. It is whatever causes the depression, physiological or psychological, that must be found and faced, and then healed… pills cannot help you discover what depression needs to tell you. On the contrary, they can mute your intuition and your inner voice…"

Back in the late '70s, when popping Prozac came into vogue, they used to be called "happy pills", as if ending depression were all it took to produce joy and spiritual fulfilment. Episodes of depression these days are seen as aberrant and downright politically incorrect, now that statisticians and elected governments generalize about what level of education, how much money, how many children and what kind of diet "should" create health and happiness in once private lives. Feeling low even with good reason is too often seen to merit medication to make it go away, never mind patience and understanding, or our ability to change ourselves, our minds and our surroundings.

Palliatives can be a merciful aid over a crisis; however, simple observation suggests that pills taken to ease the blues can easily become habitual and begin to dim the spirit and originality of pill-takers. How many masterpieces were inspired by depression or created as an escape from it? How much art and thought and charity would the world be lacking now if their creators had swallowed painkillers?

"Sometimes you do have to wonder," moans Common Sense, looking up from black headlines in her daily paper, "why anyone can be bothered to go on."

"Because to go on feeling means you give a damn," chides old Wisdom. "And to feel bad is feeling too."

11

Truth and Consequences

I had not yet learnt the words "melancholy" or "pensive". I knew only that Mother's upside-down smile and squeezed eyes meant it needed a strong tug on her skirt to turn her away from the window, where she stood watching snow fall.

"Mom, Mom," I said, and I tugged again. "Mom, Miss Hoyt told us at school today that if we don't behave ourselves Santa Claus won't bring any presents."

My mother looked down at me – she shook the otherwhere look off her face.

"There is no Santa Claus, Irma, you should know that."

Indeed, I had suspected that there was no Santa, never mind seasonal sing-songs at school or the accumulating fuss in the streets over his imminence. There had been no trace of him at home – no waving tinsel in our windows, no welcoming wreath on our door, not even a chimney for him to descend with his sack of gifts. Even should it turn out some day that there really was a Santa, he was not interested in Jewish kids. While most of our classmates were waiting at home for Santa, my little brother and I were bundled off to Grandpa Joe's house next door, where we lit Hannukah candles every night for a week and finally received a handful of coins that Grandpa Joe called "Hannukah geldt". We promised Daddy never to tell Grandpa that the coins were deposited later into little banks shaped as piggies.

I tugged my mother's skirt again.

"You are really, really sure, Mommy, there really is no Santa Claus?"

"There is no Santa Claus, Irma, believe me. Never has been, never will be. Not for us."

True, we had no Christmas tree in our living room to shelter gifts, but I had to wonder why our parents used to overact surprise on the mid-December morning when they stood in the doorway to watch my brother and me wake up in our double-decker bed and find all the wrapped packages stacked at our feet.

"Who gives us the presents, Mommy? Is it the Tooth Fairy? Is it the Wicked Witch?" I asked, as if I had not guessed her reply.

"Don't be a silly girl. Daddy and I give you the presents because we don't want you to feel left out at school the way I did when I was a little girl in Elwood, Indiana."

At last the way was open for the question I had been aiming at all along.

"Does Miss Hoyt know there is no Santa Claus?"

"Of course Miss Hoyt knows there's no Santa. Your teacher uses him to keep you all quiet and in line."

The pupils in my school descended from disparate faiths and nations, all but few of them dedicated to related gospels, so when we gathered for weekly school assemblies our Principal, Mr Guilford, could cite the Ten Commandments, confident that his audience had already learnt better than to disobey them. Mr Guilford omitted only the botanical stricture, and having overheard of it at home, I thought that was because no "addle tree" grew in any local garden.

"Mom, Mom, are you sure that Miss Hoyt knows there isn't any Santa?"

"Is that not what I just told you, Irma?"

I pictured Miss Hoyt's crumpling frown, and in my mind's ear I heard her fingers tapping the blackboard in a rhythm that I used to imitate softly on my desk so that I might feel in myself the impatience behind her staccato. For absolutely certain there was no Santa Claus: my mother said so. And that had to mean my teacher, Miss Hoyt, punctilious as she was and despite the cross at her neck, was lying. "Miss Hoyt," I said to my mother, "is a *bear* of false witness."

It was our first day back at school after the Christmas holidays.

"Miss Hoyt is fibbing," I said to Celia at the desk neighbouring mine. "There is no Santa Claus." And then I leant over to whisper in her ear: "My mother told me so."

Celia gasped. She banged her little fist on the desktop and stamped her little foot under it. "There is, too, a Santa. There is! There is too! My mommy told me so. And my mommy never tells lies!"

Celia burst into tears. I almost did too – tears of repentance for having told her the truth.

Bye-bye, Santa Claus. The Tooth Fairy was soon to be written off. The Wicked Witch was approaching the end of her days, and in due course the natal stork was going to take flight for ever. After I started to read books on my own and learn how easy it was to cross the border between reality and fiction (for example, when the Rabbit in a waistcoat led me back again to Wonderland), a precept of Common Sense was trimmed to size and put in place to size: to believe is not the same as to know – I know that two and two must always make four, but what I believe is a choice, and that is up to me. Anyone can genuinely believe what looks prettier than its alternatives and believe whatever eases confusion, envy or terror. We can believe because we are too lazy not to, and some will always put their belief in tenets and -isms designed to give them control over others. A belief is the truth only for those who choose it. Troubles set in when we grow up and start to perceive for ourselves and to question. First, is what we are seeing or being told the truth? And then, does what I hold as true need to be told to others?

"My mom says you're fat because you eat junk food at home..." a friend's little girl announced to a stout guest at their dinner table, loud enough for all of us to hear.

I had been travelling around the globe with an overnight case and a schedule ruled by impulse. It was a journey that required me often to be airborne, up there where inches are beneath contempt. And every touchdown woke again my lifelong dream of exploring the world inch by inch to make all of it my neighbourhood and its inhabitants all my neighbours. When I finally landed back in London, which had been my base for the last five years, the unexpected thrill of homecoming told me that I had become a former American: I was an expatriate. The key turned in the lock on my little bit of "The Big Smoke", my kettle was soon on the boil, and while I sorted through a hillock of post, the explorer within me finally waved "*au revoir*". I nursed a "cuppa" and then, after unpacking, I flicked through the notebook kept during my fortnight in war-torn Vietnam.

"If that was one of your traveller's dreams," said Common Sense, as I skimmed pages that dealt with drug-dealing among the soldiers in Saigon, "then you'd better wake up fast and stay awake."

"And what are nightmares," Wisdom asked, "if they are not dreams too?"

The ringing telephone interrupted my settling-in.

"Come over. Now. We need to talk," said Mimi, her New York vowels sounding to jet-lagged ears more of a warning than a welcome. "And Sandra's here too," she added, to compound apprehension.

Mimi was a friend and former classmate of mine whose husband ended their long honeymoon in Europe when he scampered back home to America. New York was not big enough for both of them, not with Pete's new girlfriend lodged there too, so Mimi stayed put in London. Her bargain rental in Chelsea had been mine before I moved to still-unfashionable Notting Hill and passed the old flat on to her, along with most of the furnishings. When I made to sit in my old rocking chair, Mimi said sharply: "No. Not there. You need to sit here at the table with Sandra and me." Then she added: "We have to talk. For your own good."

She seated herself across from Sandra at my old round table and beckoned me into the chair between them, so the window looking down into an air shaft was before my eyes.

"You know," said Mimi, "the time has come to cut your hair. Long hair makes a woman look like she's trying to cling to youth. We think you should cut it..."

Mimi's sculpted cap had gone red since the breakup of her marriage: it blazed in autumnal sunlight coming through the window.

"The truth is," said Sandra in her middle-England accent, patting her own ashy-blonde hair, "we honestly do think you should cut it."

Stung to a defence of my coif on economic if not aesthetic grounds, I said: "But..." – and then not another word.

To listen and to lay down the law are incompatible activities, and Common Sense told me that the two lawgivers who hemmed me in could not hear anything I tried to say. So I just nodded my unkempt head and let them go on and on and on about it.

While I was seeing the world, Mimi and Sandra had joined hands and hurled themselves into a branch of the fledgling "anti-psychiatry movement", established paradoxically by psychiatrists, most of them men who courted women as their followers and unpaid publicists.

"You should do it too," Mimi said, having described a group exercise designed to heal what she called "the subconscious birth trauma" by means of a wriggling re-enactment of being born. "It is truly transforming. You should come with us for your own rebirthing."

"Once was enough for me," I replied, touching off a bombardment of opinions, each one of them delivered as an ineluctable truth, about my escapist witticisms, my unwholesome preference for solitary travel, my hectic love life, my throwaway journalism – even my scrappy wardrobe. "Should" – should stop running away, should break off with the current boyfriend who was a loser, should stop interviewing celebrities for glossy magazines, should wear skirts, not trouser suits – "should", "should", "should" splattered around me. And then another word, one I had learnt in Vietnam, exploded in my mind: "fragging" – the hurling of fragmenting grenades over the heads of officers by their own enlisted men. Given the racial discrimination evidenced in the military hierarchy of that era, "fragging" was an early manifestation of America's emergent Black Power Movement.

"You should listen to us, you really should. We are telling you the truth," said Sandra. With a shattered marriage of her own not long behind her, as well as the tragedy of her infant son's death, Sandra was soon to become a force in the Women's Liberation Movement. "It's for your own good," she said.

"What you need to do now," said Mimi, "is get up from your chair and stand like this, like we are standing…"

They rose and stood to attention in the middle of the room. I rose and made to stand shoulder-to-shoulder with my dotty old friends.

"No," Mimi said. "Not like that: stand in front of us with your back to us. Like that, yes. You need to let yourself fall – just let yourself fall… fall backwards. If you trust us always to tell you the truth and nothing less than the truth, then you'll trust us to catch you. So let yourself fall backwards and prove your trust…"

"No!" It was practically the first word I had been allowed to utter. "No!"

"Are you actually saying you do not trust us?" Sandra said, and drew herself to full height in preparation for a fight. "We would never lie to you!"

"No!" I said again, and it was I who lied to save friendships for sunnier days, as well as saving my spine from possible fracture. "I mean I'm unable to do it because I strained my back very badly." And then, because weak lies require boosters, I added: "Surfing in Australia..."

Homeward-bound after a conciliatory cup of mint tea, Common Sense whispered in my ear: "Anyone can tell other people what they could do. Only doctors, lawyers or bankers can tell them what they should do. And they don't always get it right."

"The word 'should'," Wisdom added, "is short for 'because I say so'."

"Should I tell her?" starts a torrent of letters and confessions pouring through a life in agony, usually followed by concern about a friend's partner – who, more often than not, has come on to the correspondent.

"Should I tell her?" asked my young neighbour in the queue at our local post office. And she told me that she had seen the boyfriend of her best friend hugging a pretty girl in front of a local B&B. "Should I tell her? I saw it with my own eyes. And he put her in a taxi and stood there blowing kisses. It's the truth, so help me. My friend should know what a cheat he is. Don't you agree?"

We shuffled forward a few steps.

"Remember what happens to the messenger bearing bad news," I said. "She's going to tell him what you saw, and when he denies the accusation she'll believe his version. Even if he admits he was a bad boy, she may forgive him, and then you'll be the one she'll have to drop, because you know too much. And what if she does find out that he's the lying cheat you take him to be? Those poisonous words – 'I told you so' – will hang in the air around you and could destroy the friendship, which means you won't be there for your friend when she really needs a shoulder to cry on…"

A few days later, when I saw the girl running towards me on a local street, I crossed my fingers and stood my ground.

"Thank Heavens!" she said. "I didn't tell her. Because yesterday, when we met, she told me that her boyfriend's sister had come down from York. It was his sister – that's who I saw him hugging."

Lying is reckoned to be motivated by vanity, greed, lust and other certifiable vices; telling the truth is held to be pure, free from any impulse except its virtuous self.

"Good people never lie, you can bet your life on that, Irma," my maternal grandma Annie warned me when I told her that it was my little brother and not I who had trampled the marigolds in the garden. Many years later, during a long drive through the Louisiana bayou, Grandma Annie's mid-Western twang returned to mind – "You can bet your life… good people never lie…" – for I was in the act of doing just that: betting my life on a lie.

The tall man in the driver's seat pulled up at last in front of an isolated house built on stilts over swampland. I switched off my tape recorder and slipped it into my handbag. Our journey from New Orleans had been accompanied by a tirade banging on and on like the boots of a hostile army, which I was going to endure again in London when I transcribed the tapes. I stepped out of the car into spongy air and a cacophony of croaks and buzzes inspired by the setting sun. My companion led the way up to the porch of the house, where he knocked his fist hard against the door. A little old woman opened it – and even though he was barely half her age, she lowered her head in deference.

"Howdy, Jennifer," he said.

The room behind her was three times the length of its width. A dozen men wearing shirts and denim sat at a long table, and in front of a shuttered window at the far end of the room were two more men who looked up from cleaning the barrels of their rifles and waved the weapons our way in greeting. No other women were in sight, only the smell of roasting meat emanated from what had to be the kitchen next door.

"Welcome to our klavern," said my guide, and he stood to one side so I could precede him into the room where the Ku Klux Klansmen rose to welcome me and the man they called their "Grand Dragon".

"This is Miss Curtis," the Grand Dragon said. "She is here to write about us for a newspaper in England. I have been telling Miss Curtis how the Jews are the fomenters of trouble with niggers," he told the room at large. "Niggers are too stupid to be trouble. We could handle them easy if it weren't for the big-city kikes stirring them up."

"Those damn Jews!" said the white-haired woman as she reached for my coat. "I can always make out who's a Jew by the look on their faces..."

Miss Curtis from England forced a smile onto her face and decided it was a good idea not to correct the Grand Dragon's transatlantic mishearing of her surname. For the next few hours, defended by flimsy lies of omission, I listened to the Klansmen pollute the air with filth that every last one of them believed and would swear on oath was absolutely true.

"We are only servants of the truth…" said the Grand Dragon, and he signalled Jennifer to serve me first a plate of slippery pork.

Doubtful though it was that all the men in that room would be willing to die for their stinking truth, I could not doubt for one moment that every last one of them would kill for it.

History is blood-soaked by people who band together in a belief they hold as absolute truth. And being true makes what they believe supremely good. Therefore, those who oppose their belief are by definition supremely bad. Is it not the duty and purpose of good to triumph over bad? And of truth to stamp out lies? Even those who would not murder to support their belief will sacrifice the human gifts of tolerance and kindness on its behalf. Truth must be told. Or must it? And if truth be told, then who should do the telling?

The young woman wore trainers and jeans for a jog through the park. Two strangers about to become short-term intimates, we sat either side of a bench across from the duck pond. Our starting button was pushed when a pair of teenage identical twin girls strolled along the path in front of us.

"My sister's only a year younger than me," the stranger said, sliding closer to me, "and we're like a pair of twins.

At least, we used to be. She shares a flat with some friends only a few streets from where my boyfriend and I live. She always used to come over to our place. And we met up a lot at our folks' place too. But she's been staying away recently. She's gone all, like, moody, you know? Our mum asked me this morning what I thought was wrong. I told Mum I didn't know, but" – she hesitated for a moment – "I'm lying; I'm lying to my mum. I do know what's wrong. My sister told me that she's gay. I wish she hadn't told me. Because now I keep thinking: should I tell Mum and Dad the truth? I guess I really should tell them the truth…" she sighed and shook her worried head.

"It is the truth," I said. "But it's not your truth, is it? I mean it's your sister's truth. Isn't it up to her to tell your parents her own truth?"

"But I have to do something," she said. "She's making everyone so unhappy."

"Why not call your sister and ask to meet up, just the two of you, for a heart-to-heart? Do it before her silence freezes solid. She trusts you – or why would she have confided in you?" I asked, swallowing the possibility that her sister, consciously or not, might want her to tell their parents, and so lift the burden of truth from herself. "You could tell your sister that your folks know something is wrong. Most important of all, promise to stand beside her and be there for her when she feels ready to come out to them."

"Yes," my companion nodded. "Yes, I could do that. I'm going to ask my sister to meet up for a talk."

Before going my way, I dug a slice of bread out of my shopping bag to throw into the pond under the notice telling us not to feed the ducks, lest we feed hungry rats as well.

Truth is or truth ain't: lies, on the other hand, range from fibs to criminal slander. Contests of competitive fibbing are among acceptable ways to have fun, even to earn a living, as I learnt long ago at sea.

We had travelled under sail from the Isle of Wight through the Bay of Biscay and finally docked in Gibraltar. Precisely how long the journey had been, nobody on board could say. Our radio stopped functioning early on, and there was no calendar to hand, so once we lost sight of land the hours blended into one long time. Powered by wind, under instruction from stars and the horizon, we manoeuvred our wooden hull through days and nights that flowed as timeless as the sea around us. Being the delegated cook, I knew that forty-eight meals were consumed between Britain and Gibraltar, not including breakfasts caught on the run or the many times we were too buffeted by the elements to sit at table and had to stand instead, elbow to elbow, passing cups of cold tinned soup down the line.

After a break in Gibraltar, ten more meals brought us to Cannes, a congenial port town in those days. We were all flat broke – except Pete, of course. Our classic sloop was a whim he had satisfied with a few of his pretty pennies. Being owner of our craft made Pete the boss ashore, but at sea he took his orders like the rest of us from Skipper, the only experienced sailor among us wobbly amateurs. Pete's wife, Mimi, was the only other woman on board. Chronic seasickness made her unable to help in the coffin-shaped galley or to stand watch: she was seen above decks only in calm weather. An American naval fleet was moored outside Cannes harbour when we sailed in, and it was Pete, an experienced poker hand, who came up with the idea of running a game on board for the sailors: it would be fun, he said, as well as paying the mooring fee.

Most nights for a month or so between six and midnight, while our fellow crew members amused themselves ashore, Pete and I stayed on board, he to play with the punters – or to play against them – and I to cater the event. Once snacks and glasses had been arranged on a narrow sideboard in the main cabin, I was posted topside to wait until refills were required. Lights flickered ashore, and stars streamed overhead. The vast silence around me was broken only by tidal swish and the occasional bellow of triumph or profanity from below. I soon discovered that by peering down through skylights set above the main cabin I could see the hands being dealt and watch how they were played. It was an observation post that delivered a graduate course in techniques of lying. Granted, "bluff" does not smack the ear as a "lie", but what is a deception hopeful of profit if not an opportunistic lie?

During nights of play I noted the players who folded their hands when basic calculations showed they could not win. Those inveterate truth-tellers were by far fewer than fakers who raised bets on the table while transmitting signals – widened eyes, puffs of breath, lips narrowed as if to prevent a smile – to hint that they held good cards and not the rubbish visible from my vantage point. And when a gamesman's cards were strong, he affected quick frowns of uncertainty to entice others into bidding. Over and over again hands in with a chance folded in deference to talented liars – or bluffers, if you prefer. Conversation was sparse: mostly, the players were fixed, like actors waiting to be called on stage. Pete played a cerebral game, strong on arithmetic and most of all on memory. He never left the table as a loser; even while winning steadily he did not discourage the others by very often winning dramatically.

"Hey, you walk the deck at night, don't you?" Pete said one evening while I was preparing snacks for the arrival of the US Navy. "You watch through the skylights, don't you? You know, you and I could work out a code, something simple like sneezes or coughs, something like that. And then you could nip below to make more canapés or wash glasses and tip me off in code about who's holding strong cards... " Seeing my reaction, he said: "Hey, OK. I was only kidding. Forget I said it."

It was not surprising later to learn that Pete and Mimi broke up in London when she came back to their hotel room unexpectedly and found him cheating. To this day in my life of agony the image returns of salty forearms sweeping up their winnings whenever yet another communiqué begins: "He said he loved me and I believed him..." Although I myself play no games of cards or chance, it is my understanding that subtle lying is required in bridge too, the partnered game that women in general prefer to poker. I would bet my bottom dollar that we are every bit as good at bluffing as our male partners. Away from the felt-topped tables of chance, one sex has always worked bluffs on the other.

"Dear Irma, I love my boyfriend, and we are talking about living together. The problem is I lie about my orgasms. I get close to having them, but I just can't 'come' before he's all finished. I feel so inadequate. Should I tell him that I've been faking orgasms?"

"'Inadequate' does not apply. Forget the word. Orgasms are waiting for you to have them, and he is the one you want to provide them. Heat yourself up sexually when you're all alone by imagining everything you would like him to do in bed. Then when you two are alone, instead of telling him you fake orgasms and worrying him with what he will take to be his own 'inadequacy', tell him in detail all the sexy thoughts you've had and stall intercourse until you're both panting for it. During the action in bed use whispered words and ask him questions, naughty and tender to slow him down and give you time to catch up. Sexual intercourse aims for a goal – that's why it qualifies as a game as well as a drive or a duty. Play the game with zest and originality: play it for fun and play it with love. Let it be a game for life."

No women joined our on-board poker school. Years later, however, a local woman often played at a poker school in London that I catered from time to time for a male chum. Her presence at the table inhibited the language of the men, but not their tactics, and she bluffed every bit as well as the best of them, usually walking away in the money. She was one of two dedicated poker-playing women I have known. Native to different counties, the two never met or played at the same table. In the course of a boozy chat, the American told me that her dad had really wanted a son as his firstborn, and preferred her younger brothers to her. Tempted though I was, I never dared ask the Englishwoman if her case was similar.

"Stop! Stop right there," says Common Sense. "Coincidence can prove nothing more than itself."

"But collect coincidences that come your way," says Wisdom "in case you start spotting exceptions that prove them to be a rule."

12

How Do I Know?

My turban was askew again; the flimsy rag would keep snarling itself with my long earrings. Gypsy bling has never been my style, certainly not since bespectacled middle age, when glitter and glitz around my face began to make me resemble the plumed matrons who used to parade the seafront of Miami Beach. Not that anyone milling around me in our local London churchyard would make such an exotic connection. Although a number of my neighbours were not British by birth, it was doubtful that any others in the crowd were American-born, and even if one or two happened to come originally from my vast homeland, there was a less than small chance that they ever drove with their families down the north-eastern coast as we used to do every year, to spend school holidays on Florida's "South Beach", still an art-deco gem when I was a little girl, and replete with kosher restaurants to feed a flood of winter visitors from Manhattan.

Soho in London was my address now, and our annual summer fair was taking place. Food stalls set up by restaurants in China Town and Italian eateries encircled the area full of booths and wheels and bright lights of entertainment, as well as a raised stage to accommodate jazz performances from local clubs and a transvestite cabaret act from Madame Jojo's establishment nearby. Clowns and playground amusements awaited children from the local school next door.

Although the fair had just officially begun, a queue was forming in front of my tent. I hitched up my long skirt so I could slip under the back flap. I was surprised to find my first customer already installed at the round consulting table, and surprised, too, that it was a man. Over all the years I had been donating a day every summer to the charity fair, my clientele was mostly female. Men preferred not to be seen hanging around the tent of "Madame Irma" – not unless they were dragged there by partners seeking the low-down on their relationships. The lad awaiting me sat with his head cradled in his arms on the table in front of him. Was he asleep? No. He looked up wide-eyed when I entered. With a gesture of my hand I discouraged him from rising politely at my arrival into the cramped space. I smiled and seated myself in the chair across from his, putting us eye-to-eye across a puddle of red and gold brocade shawls that had been thrown across the table by the fair's organizers.

"Don't they know by now that I read palms, not bubbles? I said with a nod at the crystal ball installed inexplicably on the table top.

The furrows in the boy's forehead smoothed when he smiled; they were not yet ingrained and so must derive from something other than inherent bad temper. It was not anger, no, not anger: it was sorrow I saw festering in his wide-set blue eyes.

"Which hand do you want to read?" he asked in a tenor not long broken, still unsettled.

"Are you right-handed?"

My rudimental knowledge came out of a classic guide to palmistry I had inherited from my mother, who loved to mystify my playmates and impress their parents with her audacious predictions spun around the lines in their hands.

"The right hand shows us what is and what will be," I told the youngster. "The left hand shows us what could have been…"

His left hand clenched into a fist on the table top, and he extended the right hand to me. The lithe hand I held in mine was mildly callused from gripping a cricket bat, was my guess. The boy's forehead creased again – his mouth bit inwards to contain hope, perhaps? Or laughter? No. It was not laughter bubbling within his slender frame.

"Your head line is long and strong," I told him. "It's uncluttered by nonsense. You have a rare ability to concentrate: you know how to direct your attention. You're not one to be distracted, are you? Not when your goal is in sight – that's for sure. And you really enjoy competition, yes, you like competing to a sporting degree…"

His hand trembled suddenly and wanted to pulled away. I switched fast to anodyne observations – first about money: a steady supply awaited him; and then there was future travel over water, which is always a safe prediction for any palmist at work in a nation composed of islands.

"May I see both hands now, side by side?" I said. "The left hand too, the one that shows what could have been."

Here I must make memory conditional. Did I see the jagged break, a near-mortal interruption that occurred early in the boy's long lifeline? Or is recollection making itself subservient to palmistry? Cunning and witless though palmistry is, it nevertheless can offer explanations easier to defend than those deriving from intuition. Intuition is deemed illogical even by people who possess it to a rare degree.

"Your life" – I hesitated before committing myself to a statement that one way or another without doubt I knew to be a fact – "your life was interrupted by a trauma. I mean that something bad, something bad and unexpected happened to you. And it happened not very long ago."

He closed his eyes and took a deep breath to still the tremor of his heart.

"Listen to me," I said, fixing my gaze on his palms outstretched before me side by side as pages in an open book and speaking slowly, as if reading words written upon them. "You are strong. You are a strong young man, strong of heart and strong of mind. Your life has suffered a radical shake-up, yes, true enough. But not only will your heart and soul heal and resume their course, they will grow stronger and stronger and stronger. And your head line is very strong too. Look: see? This is your head line. Can you see how straight it runs? How determined it is? You are going to do a lot more, young man, than just overcome the dreadful thing that happened to you. When the healing ends, as it will soon end, your progress will become deep and creative. Every day you are gaining strength. Success lies ahead of you."

"Do you see it? Do you see success?"

"I do," I said. And so I did. "A profession is calling you. The arts?..." I glanced up and suggested: "Or science? Or maybe you're going to make your name in a business venture? Your hand is still too young to tell me what your life's work is going to be. Worldly decisions of that sort are up to your mind and your inclination to determine first, before there is any evidence to read in your palm. But I certainly see a successful path opening soon, very soon. Unusual achievement is on the cards for you. And, oh yes..." I turned his hand and squeezed it to reveal lines on its side, "Oh yes, you will be loved. Oh my, yes!"

"Will I? Will I be loved?"

"Indeed you will," I studied the lines. "Naughty boy! And loved at last by someone whose respect for you is equal to" – before selecting a pronoun I checked his eyes for a flicker of straight lust as I had learnt to do when reading palms at the Soho fair – "her... passion. And now, will you be kind enough to cross my palm with silver? Or drop it straight into this collection box for our local charity."

He reached into the pocket of his jacket for clattering coins. Then he turned his head and called out: "Dad!"

A stocky older version of the boy put his head through the entrance flap of the tent. He nodded at me before he turned away to enter backwards, pulling a wheelchair. Only when the older man lifted his son bodily to transfer him to the wheelchair did I see that the boy's legs were severed at his knees.

"Thank you," he said when he was settled in his chair. "Thank you so much. The doctors say they can fit me with legs. And maybe I'll learn to dance on them."

Never before had any charlatan received a reward as valuable as the smile he gave me.

Examining strangers' palms while holding their open hands in mine encouraged intuition to assert itself. As the hours drew on, I found myself reading more than the lines before me: more and more was revealed in a manner fleet and fleeting and too airy-fairy for analysis. Many of the revelations that were not immediately explicable were explained later at leisure by Common Sense. While I commented pedantically on the hands I held, clues were fluttering around the subjects: there were pale circles where wedding rings were no longer, tresses dyed purple over grey roots and sharp nails painted the colour of blood; above them faces bespeaking rage, disappointment, weary depression and sometimes aglow with hope. I looked up from pontificating on the heart line of one pretty young spinster to see her turn swiftly and glance behind her precisely the way an acquaintance of mine did at any mention of love. Was it a safe guess that her secret too was a married man? Whereupon she turned back to me, and in her troubled eyes I saw that, no, it was not a married man she loved. Odds on, it was another woman.

When scientists and other dedicated fact-finders stormed the ancient territory of prophets and soothsayers, they built citadels of their own along the road to eternal life. These rational constructs are lofty, and some of them are thick too. Granted, they exclude nonsense from our daily life; however, they can also cast our appetites and our dreams into the shade, and dim the light of love by claiming to explain it. Earthbound science and its attendant robot, technology, threaten to enslave us as earlier dogmas did and still do, by pinning us to general rules about what is good and what is bad – not just for our bodies: for our spirits too.

"We are not in the realm of logic any more: we are in the realm of emotion," said a scientist interviewed recently on the radio, brushing off his interviewer's question regarding motives behind some of the research into genetics.

"Logic and emotions! If they are incompatible, then so is everything and everyone else!" Wisdom and Common Sense cry out in harmony.

An alert traveller well along the bumpy road to Wisdom has encountered many different facial types among our human species and will have observed that there are only so many of them. Strangers who pass before old, experienced eyes bring back images of others whom they resemble in bone structure and tint of skin. Only the design imprinted upon each face from within is impossible to read or typecast at a glimpse, and it is this handiwork of an individual's thought and hope and feeling that captivates intuition. Intuition flits around the borders of logic and it is bothersome to pin down, so there will for ever be people who try to boil it down instead into palmistry, astrology, clairvoyance, faith, numerology or fashionable "body language". Call intuition guesswork, call it analysis, call it a hunch, or call it "digging the vibe", as hippies used to do – whatever you call it, even call it crazy – intuition qualifies as our sixth sense. And as the other senses, the sixth one is animal too by nature. Nor is the sixth sense independent of the other five: how could it be? Our sensual impressions of sight, sound, taste, smell and touch overlap each other while each remains itself. And Wisdom never dismisses evidence delivered by any one of our senses, including the sixth of them. Maybe some day scientists will deign to investigate the way we can know so much in a flash beyond proof or before it. If the boffins do get around to researching intuition, I hope they call me as a witness.

Not one bird was to be seen flying over Auschwitz more than forty years ago when I went to see for myself that corner of hell on earth. I was alone, the only living soul in a desert of wasted life where the sky was grey in spite of autumn sunshine, salt stung the inland air, and the throb of keening beat beneath what only my ears heard as silence.

Many years later similar dour contradictions pervaded an island I was visiting off the western coast of Africa. Upon my return to the mainland I was not surprised to be informed that captives used to be held on the island before their long journey across the sea into slavery, a voyage many did not survive – and how many others wished they had not?

When I say that a stocky stranger followed me out onto the deck of the cross-Channel ferry boat, I mean only that his exit from the crowded salon happened to be on the heels of mine: we had not made eye contact previously.

"This is awfully windy," he said, leaning next to where I leant on the rail. "Normally, I fly."

He was Canadian, he told me, when I asked the provenance of his accent, as we North Americans always do when we overhear each other on the road. A long-time resident of Paris, he was on his way back there now from a business trip to London. Men introduce themselves in the same manner they define themselves, by what they do for a living, so I could pose the question still rarely put to a woman upon first meeting: "What do you do?"

"Me?" he said. "I'm a nose. I'm a professional nose."

A covert glance at the organ he referred to showed it as snub and nondescript. Was he joking? He was looking out to the horizon and not at me as he would have been to see an expected smile, were his words intended to be funny.

"I've heard of private eyes. But a professional nose? That's a new one on me. What does a nose do?" I asked.

His practised tone made it clear I was not the first person to whom he had explained that professional noses are employed by manufacturers of perfumes and beauty products to assess their wares, as well as those of their competitors, so they can then make changes or additions. Thanks to a preternatural sense of smell, professional noses are able to sniff out the ingredients of an aroma in even the most subtle combinations.

"I call it diag*nosing*," he said, and he glanced my way this time to watch me get the joke.

There on the windy deck it occurred to me that among the other five senses informing our instincts, the sixth sense resembles smell. Intuition's material arrives in whiffs and sniffs – and sometimes in a full blast that the receiver cannot ignore or escape. Intuition is redolent of memories as aromas are too; the products of intuition cannot be snapped or tasted, making them difficult to compare, and they are far more difficult even than perfume to reproduce via a recipe.

"Do you," the professional nose began, and noting my white hair he asked: "still work?"

"My job is a bit like yours," I said. "I'm a professional ear, a professional ear with a big mouth."

I hoped he had not noticed that I had inadvertently inched downwind of him after learning the nature of his profession. Employment of a rare faculty makes for lonely work.

Before "use by" dates relieved our noses of their life-saving duty, and long before our senses became dedicated primarily to pleasure, human beings used to rely upon them (including the sixth one), as all other animals do, for sustenance and safety. My brother is a doctor of medicine, a man of intellect and science; nevertheless, he had to agree – albeit with a bemused smile – that even though intuition is commonly referred to as "feminine", in childhood (before rules and regulations are taken to heart) it beats strong in both genders.

Daddy enjoyed congenial shopping in the hardware store-cum-filling station near our house in the country, so my little brother and I knew he was going to be ages as usual. We were waiting obediently in the car, which was parked in the lane. To the right of us, woodland rose to the top of a mountain; on our left was a footpath under birch trees down to where we could see the lake sparkle in sunshine. The only house in sight was about halfway to the shoreline: a tumbledown log cabin set back from the path. No smoke was rising from its lopsided chimney, and the front garden was overgrown with rippling weeds. My brother and I looked at each other: we giggled, and then we jumped out of the car to skip side by side down the trail to open water. As we were passing the cabin, its door flew open. The man who emerged was tall and roughly bearded. He was dressed in greens and greys topped by a hunter's hat.

"Hello, kids," he called out. "How you kids doin'? Wanna have some fun?"

This was a small country community, where folks were friendly and strangers were made welcome. So why did my brother and I not reply: "Hello, sir"? Why did we stop cold, exchange a look and grab each other's hands?

"Hello, kids…" he said again.

He started ambling towards us. I heard his smile hissing like a marksman's "yes" when a deer comes into range. My brother and I turned as one, hand in hand we ran back up the hill, and then into the car as fast as we could.

"He's a bad man," my brother said, after we were safely settled with the door locked from inside.

"He's a bad man," I agreed.

Neither of us mentioned the creepy event to our father – how could we? We had no acceptable proof to offer a grown-up for what we both had known was true, nor did we ever speak of it again to each other until more than a half-century later, when my brother and I agreed that mutual intuition had saved our innocence, if not our very lives, on the country path.

If the atavistic sixth sense has settled into us females stronger and deeper than into males, that must be thanks to the exercise it had protecting us and our cradled young from aggressive, bigger creatures. How often, when walking in Uptown Manhattan alone or with another girl, did we cross

an ill-lit street to avoid the oncoming figure our joint intuition marked as a predator? Nowadays pretty young ears are
plugged into headsets on the road, and girls together on our
dark streets are not so often talking to each other as each is
talking into a mobile gizmo. Oncoming figure? What oncoming figure? Old hands in a life of agony can but hope that
fewer menacing figures are abroad these days, when the creeps
can choose to stay home and visit porn sites for virtual kicks.

There can be no question that the human genius for engineering and technology has lifted us out of the mud in more
ways than one. The invention of indoor plumbing, vacuum
cleaner, refrigerator and domestic washing machine remain
every bit as imperative to the liberation of women as the vote
and the pill. And, as usual, there will be a price to pay as our
old skills (and pleasures too) left unpractised must lose their
edge and cease to be passed down through generations, until
like languages unspoken they go into decline and disappear.

My little brother clapped his hands and shouted: "Wahoo!"

"Shush," I warned him from my superior status of nearly
twelve years old. "Shut up and watch."

None of our friends had a television set. Ours was the very
first "goggle box" in the community where we spent summer

holidays. Dad had fitted a big free-standing magnifying glass in front of the screen so all four of us could watch it side by side on the sofa, my brother and I squeezed between our parents.

"This is amazing," said our Dad while we watched a tropical hurricane whip waves sky-high and dry in front of our eyes. "The whole world has come home to us."

Indeed, the whole world was ours in black and white. Home life was soon pushed aside by the lives of strangers, foreign as well as fictional. Before the summer was over, our quarrelsome games of Monopoly were abandoned in favour of cartoons on the box, and we kids never again dressed up in homemade costumes to act out impromptu tales for our applauding parents. It was not long before dinner ceased to be a noisy circular event around the table: instead, we took meals in horizontal silence, plates on our laps, all together and each alone in front of the television set.

"Have problems changed much during your life in agony?" countless interviewers and curious strangers have asked over the years.

"The media of communication have changed radically," is my reply, "and like the man said" – a quick check to make sure the questioner might have heard of "the man" – "Marshall

McLuhan it was, who said back in the 1960s: 'The medium is the message.' And it turned out to be truer than we knew at the time. The medium has surpassed the message. These days the medium tailors the message to its own dimensions."

At the start of my life in agony, and for decades afterwards, correspondence used to arrive via snail mail and, as most of the letters were handwritten, it was not long before I became a self-taught graphologist. My intuition had material to work with: it could spot frames of mind in the tilt of script, personal characteristics in the chosen colour of ink and the stationery – be it formal and embossed with a return address or pale pink with an imprinted kitten looking up from the corner. Sometimes a whiff of perfume arose from the envelope and tears often blotted the words. Even typewritten letters contained underlining, strategic or impulsive, to help create a telling patina. I needed only hold the paper up to a light in order to see through crossings-out in ink or typed Xs and so read what the writer wished were not true. Letters six or seven pages in length often used to end: "Even if you cannot reply thanks anyway. I see the problem clearer now it's written down."

Practically all modern agony arrives by text or email, no backhand, no forehand, no underlining or exing out, no stamp or thoughtful walk to the postbox – simply a tap: "Send". Central issues continue to be wounded self-esteem, timid self-knowledge, sexual jealousy or frustration, hurt parading as anger and anger turned inwards as guilt. However, the individuality of the writer, the very special self that rouses and inspires an agony aunt's intuition can be subverted by a speedy, samey style of telling.

Ageing intuition works across the ever-broadening board of memory. And intuition is sniffing a new fear among young women who are delivered at last into a field of choices that can be a jungle too. There seems to be increasing fear among those who contact me of discovering their own singular selves: a growing fear in young women of individuality. Where do I find a Band-Aid for heartbreak? many appear to ask. What pill can I take for my bad marriage? Heart's quandary is reduced to a crossword clue requiring the solution – one and only – that suits the problem instead of suiting the singular one who suffers it.

I shudder to hear the pop phrase "role model", with its implied subjugation of discovery and originality to an established example, usually a celebrity, proposed as smart to imitate. I must wonder sometimes if among the sharp senses and instincts we share with other animals we are not in danger of sacrificing intuition with its roots and purpose in individuality. But on good days long emails come my way containing information about the writer, not just her problem – even a few hard-copy letters too, not all of them from correspondents over forty. Especially impromptu agony-laden talks with strangers on the road help me believe and hope that there will be a switch back to our hard-won entitlement to be each of us unique – unique in our agony too.

"Dear Irma," writes one half of a match made a million miles from heaven, "I've been miserable ever since my relationship broke up a year ago. But at last I met the perfect guy. We made contact on a dating website a few months ago, and we have been in touch every day since then. He lives in Aberdeen, which is far away from where I live. But he wants us to meet. He says he'll send me a ticket and he'll meet me at the station. My friends think I'm crazy. But I think I am really in love with him… Confused."

"Dear Confused," I reply. "Nobody can fall in love with a man she has never smelt. And you have not been within sniffing distance of this guy. So before you dream or daydream of loving him, you need to see him, to hear him, to smell him – and to suss him out. Only then, after you know him eye-to-eye and nose-to-nose, can your inner voice, the voice of intuition, inform desire and judgement. And please, be smart and promise to make the first meeting on your own territory in broad daylight…"

The sixth sense, like the others, is easily fuddled by drink and drugs, which make everything smell like roses until it ends up smelling like shit. And intuition has a dedicated enemy in hope's impersonator: wishful thinking. Wishful thinking throws a blanket over honesty, and modern methods of communication increase its threat by putting opportunistic lying beyond the reach of our senses, including the sixth sense, intuition.

"Stop kvetching," interrupts Wisdom. "Time and science run on track. But the human psyche moves in spirals and circles. Nine times out of ten, what has gone around will come around again."

"You're repeating yourself," Common Sense interrupts.

"And you too will learn to repeat yourself," replies her senior relative, "because nobody ever listens to us the first time."

13

Where Did I Put My Keys?

"Welcome back, Irma," said the immigration official.

He examined the American passport, which was still my only travel document. Frowning, he handed it back across the counter.

"Isn't it about time you came home?"

I looked around the heaving airport that had not long before been renamed Kennedy in honour of the assassinated president, and I heard myself repeat in a quizzical tone: "Home?"

The word circled my mind without a place to roost. "Home" had not attached to spiky Paris during my time there, and even though I had at last put down the roots that made London "home", the word could never have its seed or origin there for me. Now I was on my first visit back to the United States in almost a decade. The crowd in the airport was motley and unfamiliar, their accents rang alien. The oversized vehicles waiting outside the arrival door looked strange and exotic.

I no longer knew my homeland – only remembered it as it used to be.

A lot of people believe us all to be descended from a couple of disobedient expatriates and to owe our very existence to their expulsion from Eden. Others maintain that our ancestors were nomadic bipeds who sheltered in caves and trees until they finally settled down to build scattered communities that became our various homelands. When early explorers set out on ships to survey uncharted territories, most of them were in pursuit of wealth and conquest and hoped to sail back some day triumphant to their home ports. But distances being greater and elements fiercer than they ever dreamed, many died at sea or in hostile lands. Others set up colonies in places that were outlandish then; now they are just next door.

Involuntary expatriation was one of the brutal side-effects of slave-trading. And enforced expatriation was a sentence delivered upon miscreants by powerful states ousting their unwanted to remote places such as Australia and Siberia. Expatriation has always been chosen too as a flight for life: only skim a telephone directory in any American city to find an alphabetical history of famine and persecution around the world. Artists often abandon home on the trail of a muse who generally leads them to a better climate. And so often in history has expatriation been aggressive and military that to this day the uprooted can be treated as invaders of the others' homelands, even if they have arrived hungry or in pursuit of a dream. Retired people from one nation often face frigid snobbery when they up sticks to another nation's villages or seaside towns. And, of course, throughout human history many a bridge has been burnt in the wake of love.

It was one afternoon a week or so ago. I arrived early at the cinema, and when the stranger plunked herself down next to me without so much as a question or apology, I cast a look of longing at all the empty seats surrounding us.

"It's a hard life," she said to launch her spiel. "He loves me and I love him. We've been together now for almost two years, and we've both been married." Before I had a chance to ask, she answered: "I have two children, a boy and a girl. They're married now, with families of their own. He only has one daughter. She's in her twenties; she lives with her mother in Texas. He isn't British. I mean, he's American" – she gave me a look – "like you…" she said, a deduction that surprised me, as I had said not one accented word, until I reminded myself that decades of a published life in agony makes for former readers who are older than current ones and still manage to recognize me from the ancient photo over my byline. "He has to go back there in a few months, back to Texas for his work. He's asked me to marry him and live there with him in… is it El Paso? I do love him. But I don't know. I just do not know. That's why I've come to the cinema this afternoon, to give myself a chance to be alone and think."

Few women of any age ever go alone to a cinema, and fewer still undertake the outing as I often do as a distraction from confusion or the doldrums. I looked at my neighbour with interest: she was billowing and bright blonde, manicured and well painted, although no longer in her first youth; her eyes showed her as foxy and flirtatious.

"You do know that if you marry him," I said, "you'll have to marry Texas too. Don't you think you ought at least to take a look at the place? Get the feel of it before you move there to live. El Paso is not the biggest town in Texas, and you say he has his ex-family there. As they'll be on your doorstep, it would be a good idea to meet them in advance of a wedding. Don't you agree? Why not go to Texas with him on a long holiday? See how you get on with his home state and his family before you tie the knot to all of them? It's a shame we're here to see a thriller, not a western..." were my final words before the lights dimmed.

"I'm scared of flying..." were hers.

Most expatriates who contact me in my life of agony have not chosen their condition, but were delivered into it via birth to families originating abroad. Newborn expats are subject to imported rules and customs at home that can be difficult, even dangerous to bridge with local life, especially when the divide concerns romance and commitment, as those that come my way generally do.

"We met at university in Manchester, and from the first moment we united," writes the young woman. "He is starting medical training and I am studying law. We are both of Indian origin, but we are going to stay in England, where we both grew up. The trouble is my family moved here a long time before I was born, but his arrived more recently, and a lot of his close relatives are still abroad. During summer break he took me to India to meet his uncles and grandparents. They were welcoming, and I thought everything was great. And then he told me his parents got a letter saying I am not of a suitable caste to be his wife. It worried them, and they worry him. I feel upset and angry too..."

"You and he are both resident in another place and different time from the one of your mutual origins. Your commitment to each other, as well as commitment to a new way of living, has to mean breaking away from the past and detaching yourselves from a history that he was born closer to than you. The struggle therefore must be harder for him. He requires your tender and patient support. And his parents need to keep on meeting you, to know you better and better, and to see you as a strong, trustworthy link to the future. Maybe some day his distant relatives, at least the younger ones, will come to terms with your marriage. However, that they never will accept you as his worthy wife is a risk you both will run after you marry. As much as you are lovers, you must also be allies in a battle against the past…"

It was the best I could say before referring her to a local agency that helps those who find their hearts squeezed between ways of here and ways of there.

I finally left my homeland once and for all to head for bohemian Paris, where I expected free choice and creativity to be awaiting me – and where, only incidentally, I thought my unknown soulmate probably would turn up. Anyone who seeks treasures on the road must travel light and leave the frivolous extras at home. One encumbrance I rid myself of on board the ship that was carrying me to Europe was my virginity. As accommodation was cheap, it required cabins to be shared by strangers, so I abandoned my maidenhead in a lifeboat that was tied to the railing of an upper deck.

Jean-Pierre was French, of course. Frenchmen were reputed to be the world's most accomplished lovers. It seemed a good idea to begin my love life with one of them, especially one who was handsome and spoke decent English. The only girl in my college who had managed to snare herself a French boyfriend was the envy of us others. At least her good luck spurred some of us to learn the rudiments of the language. Later in Paris, after a few days sharing the tiny flat where Jean-Pierre purported to be writing a novel, he showed me a pile of love letters from a dozen American girls – among them two other virgins seduced during his brief stay in my homeland. He laughed – I left. Years later, I caught sight of Jean-Pierre through the window of a Parisian bus taking me to work. He was dressed in nondescript fashion favoured by local shopkeepers. Bald and pale and gloomy, he gripped the arm of a fractious toddler while they waited for the light to change.

"And so the future serves us right," says Common Sense.

"Or wrong," says Wisdom. "It depends on how we serve the future."

I had been more than a year in Paris when a Left Bank acquaintance, Jean-Christophe, extended what was to be my only ever invitation to a local sit-down dinner party. J.C. needed a "beard" – was how he put it – to hide his homosexuality from our hosts, a married couple resident in a posh area of Paris who were friends of his parents. He requested me please to speak no French so he could serve as my interpreter. When he told me that we were requested to arrive earlier than other guests, I figured that had to be so the hostess could size up his "Yankee girlfriend" and send a report to his folks in Montpellier.

A trim woman smartly dressed and subtly bejewelled received us at the door, where for the first time I felt myself surveyed with Right Bank approval. Instead of my usual scruff, J.C. had borrowed a silky garment from the fashion house where he worked. He even bought me new shoes, and he wove my shaggy mane into a crown of braids, still a classic coif in the early '60s, if not quite *à la mode*. Our hostess ushered us into a salon with an adjoining alcove, where I saw a table laid for six. She gestured J.C. and me to an overstuffed sofa while she hurried to answer the ringing telephone in the hall. It was only a few minutes before fashionable heels sounded her return. Shaking her head and smiling in rueful amusement, she said that her husband had rung to say an emergency had come up at work. He was desolated: he would not be able to join us in time for dinner. A shrug of padded shoulders and she removed one setting from the table to stow it in a towering carved sideboard, before excusing herself again, I assumed, to put the finishing touches to the meal.

"Everyone knows that her husband has a bit on the side," Jean-Christophe whispered in the mixture of my faltering French and his Americanized English that served our conversations. "That's why Monsieur will be turning up late tonight. But his wife, you see, she is a true Frenchwoman. And a Frenchwoman understands the needs of men. Her hubby's hanky-panky never bothers a Parisienne the way it does less sophisticated women."

I nodded my head in reluctant agreement, having read *The Second Sex*, in which Simone de Beauvoir declares adultery an acceptable pastime for both genders. And not even Jean-Paul Sartre dared disagree with de Beauvoir – why should he? The dictum must have pleased him at least as much as it did her, his off-and-on partner. Everyone everywhere – even those who did not claim to be existentialists – knew that Frenchmen were reputed to enjoy the making and taking of love wherever it popped up – and of course, French wives accepted with equanimity the sexual meandering of their menfolk.

Before our hostess could return, I excused myself to smarten up my make-up, or so I told J.C.. In fact, I was nosey. From the few glimpses I had been allowed into local homes, it was my impression that Parisians dedicated to interior décor barely a fraction of the taste and money they poured into their wardrobes on public display. The wide staircase was roughly carpeted; the paintings on the walls, most of them old portraits, were overwhelmed by massive frames; a glance through the open door of the master bedroom showed a mess of cushions and dark curtains that were drawn across the windows, which I knew must already be shuttered: the clatter of drawing shutters resonated throughout residential streets of Paris every nightfall. And then my survey stopped cold. I saw our hostess slumped over a frilled dressing table. Her head was cradled in her arms and her shoulders were shaking with sobs. I retreated fast, lest she look up to see my reflection in her mirror. And I hurried back downstairs over fragments of a crumbling myth.

When I was not earning a daily baguette by teaching English to bored locals, I spent many free hours on the terraces of Left

Bank cafés, where for the price of a single coffee I sat undisturbed by importunate waiters while the flow of life in Paris passed in front of my eyes like a fast train I lacked a ticket to board. Once in a while, as a Frenchman was walking by, he granted me an automatic assessment, cool and measuring, without a trace of the warmth or imagination exhibited by Italian men encountered on my European travels.

Eventually I landed on a small dumpy café near my cheap hotel, which turned out to be a hangout for bohemian expatriates. Although a few Frenchmen stumbled into the premises, I was never going to encounter any unaccompanied Parisian woman of my age. The only local female always in attendance was perched high up behind a till at the end of the bar, and La Patronne was not open to conversation with anyone. She gave me barely a glimmer of recognition, even after I had qualified as a regular. Although Madame was only in her forties, she was already wrinkled. Only her hair was solid black and never a strand out of place.

"Because it's a wig," explained another alien regular, a poet on the run from home in Ireland. He told me that after the war Madame was accused of having consorted with Nazi invaders. Her head was shaven, and she was then beaten through the streets with the other bald women judged guilty of the same transgression. Madame's hair never grew back again.

"I have to wonder," says Common Sense, "how often the same crime is committed for different motives?"

"That's why true justice must consider if all those who commit the same crime deserve the same punishment," says Wisdom.

The only public amenity in my Left Bank hangout was a hole in the ground. Literally. It worked well enough for men, while making women's needs barely an afterthought. To this day there are cafés to be found in France with but a single unisex loo, which means that upon leaving her cubicle a woman can be confronted by a man in the process of relieving himself in the urinal, an oxymoronic confrontation, as his back is probably turned her way. Is similar sexist superiority enacted in French bedrooms? My first-hand experience of Parisian lovemaking was inferior to my expectations. Local feeding habits, however, were everywhere on view. There are striking affinities in the manner we design to satisfy our primary animal appetites. Unlike my native New York, where it has ever been the woman who picks fussy bones about the menu before giving her order to the waiter, in Paris it was and it still is the man. The majority of French chefs of haute cuisine are men. I would bet none of them does the cooking at home. Family food has always been prepared by the housewife – "*femme au foyer*" – even if she also holds down a daytime job. And so we see the proliferation in modern France of ready-cooked meals, fast-food outlets and supermarket chains, not to mention the French branches of Weight Watchers.

Husbands were rarely to be seen doing domestic stocking-up in the old street markets of France. Nowadays, the men might push the trolleys while their womenfolk fill them from the supermarket shelves; more likely, they stand to one side, jingling car keys and wearing the mask of resignation peculiar to blokes waiting outside women's changing rooms.

James was an Englishman who worked for the Paris bureau of a national English newspaper. Older than most of us, he was a heavy drinker to be seen most nights propping up the bar until La Patronne chased him out with the rest of us so she could close the place up. One night James turned to me at the bar where I was as usual trying to make a glass of cheap red wine last as long as possible, and he asked if I would like to have a complimentary ticket for a performance of *King*

Lear that was being put on in the Paris Opera House by the English National Theatre, with Paul Scofield in the lead.

"It's a freebie. But I don't want it," James said. "I've seen more Lears in my time than I've leered at French tarts..."

Having begun to clock the verbal playfulness of British expats, if not yet the dark emotions that could be hidden under them, I smiled an eager "Yes, please". Of course I felt I had to stand James his next drink, a costly courtesy he mercifully turned down, and then offered me another glass of plonk.

On the appointed night, walking to the Place de l'Opéra, my eyes were as usual pinned to the pavement ahead of me in hope of spotting a one-punch metro ticket discarded by a tourist who did not know they were valid for day-return journeys. The City of Light had started to dim for me by that time, every day a little dimmer in the shadow of my oncoming thirtieth birthday. It was after the performance of *King Lear*, as I was walking back under the stars – while perfect words that had been delivered perfectly still worked in my heart – it was then, for the very first time, it occurred to me that if I finally abandoned Paris I did not have to take myself back across the Atlantic. What if I crossed the Channel instead? What if I went to live where the glorious language came from?

Of course, I brushed the idea aside as yet another impractical romance. However, it kept reoccurring during sleepless nights ahead, while I lay wondering whether the time had come to ask my parents for the fare home – and so run up a debt that would be repayable only at the price of my dreams and the sacrifice of my freedom.

"Dear Irma, I am so confused. I think I'm going crazy. I don't know what to do. Should I?... Shouldn't I?..."

Whether it is an importunate man who shoves a woman into the whirlpool of yes, no, stay, go, stop, start – whether it concerns having a baby or changing jobs, or if she is in conflict over undergoing cosmetic surgery – whatever her quandary, my recommendation is: first, to avoid friends or family members who are urging her towards a decision that she alone must accommodate and live with; second, to learn every practical detail available about the decision she is considering; and finally, to escape the scene of confusion, if only for long walks in parks, so that time and distance can finally lift her to a whole new view of the dilemma and its horns.

"We don't make the big decisions: the big decisions make us," says Common Sense.

"But we must let them do it," says her older colleague, Wisdom.

"Clean your plate, young lady," my mother used to tell me back in the 1940s, when food stamps and mild rationing were in place in America. "Eat every bite, because little children in England are starving. They're not as lucky as you."

How the hateful green beans on my plate could feed unlucky children in a faraway land puzzled me. Evidently luck was not logical. Good luck required me to eat every disgusting bean in front of me, while bad luck deprived other children of them. The memory of those hungry children returned to my mind twelve years later upon first sight of England. The ship carrying my student tour to Europe barely paused in Southampton, tying up not even long enough for passengers to disembark before we sped on to Le Havre.

"Everything is small in England…" I scribbled in my notebook from the ship's deck where I stood looking down. "The houses are small. They drive small cars, and the people look very small too…"

Only on our return journey, having "done" France, Germany and Italy, did our student group spend three days in London, where bomb damage was still evident, unlike Paris, where all was pristine. Horse-drawn carts still to be seen in London streets were doing daily work and not for tourists to hire. In central London men wore dark suits and bowler hats, and they carried black umbrellas too, just as they did in the old British movies. Although London at first sight could not approach my yearning vision of Paris, from the top of a double-decker bus I spotted blue plaques here and there that took my breath away and put celebrities of literature in the seat next to me. Only much later, after I had lived in London for some time, would the capital reveal itself to me as a collection of villages, each with byways and winding alleys into its own history and all within the great history of "The Big Smoke".

English acquaintances acquired here and there on the road came through for me when I finally turned up to live in their homeland. With the help of a man with whom I had shared a long, impromptu conversation years earlier at the Bull Run in Pamplona and then met accidentally in a pub not long after my arrival in London, I found the job that was going to lead me eventually to Fleet Street and journalism. My first residence was a small B&B near Marble Arch. The landlady was an addict of *The Archers* on the radio; the theme from that eternal series will ever be accompanied in my ear by the clink of big old coins demanded by the metre that controlled heating for my room.

It was not very long before a girl I met at work offered me the low-rental flat she no longer needed. It was just off the King's Road, which was the pole London had just begun to swing on in the 1960s. Despite a fair knowledge of French, I had made not one chum among Parisian women, and woman-to-woman friendship was a happy surprise in London. The sisterly connections also stirred up my life in agony again there in swinging London, where women were risking a sexual freedom that was more audacious than anywhere in Europe or America. Arrogance and aloofness were still ascribed abroad to the Brits – unfairly, or so it seemed to me, for I discovered instead modesty among them that was not far from self-denigration. The flow of apologies heard in the underground, on the streets and in every queue – "sorry," "sorry", "sorry" – alien to my New York and Parisian experience, was echoed in the agonized confessions of my new English friends and of strangers too. "What possessed me? What did I do wrong? What should I have done?" began countless tales of local heartbreak, as very many still do.

"You want to live in London!" exclaimed one of my first London cabbies. To this day I regularly encounter his incredulity from locals when they learn the provenance of my accent.

"You lived in Paris, so tell me something, honestly: is it true that Frenchmen are the best in bed as everyone says they are? Are they really better lovers than anyone else? Is that true?" asked the photographer who had recently become my first English boyfriend.

I handed him his cup of tea and sat down at table across from him.

"So they say," I told. "At least, so Frenchmen say. To be honest, I wouldn't know. But I am sure of one thing: I know I'd rather have breakfast with an Englishman."

"I've been considering running an advice column of sorts," said the male editor of the avant-garde magazine that employed me at the end of the '60s. "I thought we could make it upmarket and heavy on emotions. Would you be interested in writing it?"

My work until then had been reportages, travel writing and celebrity interviews, with only occasional "think pieces", as journalists called opinionated articles about sentiments, rela-tionships and behaviour at large. So I assumed he was having me on.

"Sure," I said, and then, having made myself at home in local banter: "why don't we call the column 'Speculum: The Way in'."

He laughed: "I should have known you'd say something like that."

So I set out, as scheduled, to interview Tennessee Williams. And my professional life in agony was postponed for five years.

A few days ago I went strolling in a London street market popular with tourists and I stopped for a quick lunch in a gastro pub. When I took my sandwich and cold drink out onto the terrace, I saw only one seat to spare. It was at a table where a couple were already installed: the girl was scrolling photos on her mobile phone, while the much older man next to her, who had to be her grandfather, sat looking around in a way that marked him as a tourist. Something about his gaze, acquisitive and comparing, suggested he was American. He gave a white-haired nod of OK when I asked if I might join them, and he said "Yeah, sure, be our guest" in inimitable New Yorkese. I saw the sausage and fries on a plate before him, and something possessed me to sing under my breath: "Pickle in the middle…" He looked up with a laugh and sang back at me: "With the mustard on the top…"

The girl raised her eyes, and her nose wrinkled in distasteful confusion that turned into revulsion when her granddad and I both sang out loud: "Just the way you like them, and they're always hot…"

"What's with you, Grampa? What are you shouting about?" she said in the modern American accent that sounds more West Coast anonymous these days than regional.

"You wouldn't know if we told you, honey," he replied.

And he was correct. Not a soul except for us two in the crowded market would know the theme of the hot-dog salesman from Jack Benny's comedy hour, a hit show on radio in an America that is no more, only its echo in the memories of momentary compatriots of an old time like the white-haired man and me.

Thus do expatriates become each of us a diminutive nation with borders defended by heaps of recollected images and doggerel, lullabies and ditties, all of which are alien not only to neighbours in the land that is not our birthplace, but alien also to younger generations everywhere, even those we love, who stand to inherit our goods more worldly.

"Oh, Mum," my London-born son used to correct me when I forgot for a moment where I was, "we're walking on a pavement, not a sidewalk."

To be an expatriate doubles the "what if" that attaches to every life as its choices age into a past and imperfect tense: "What if I had…" – "What if I had not…" And then for the expats there is always the subtext: "What if I had stayed there where I was meant to be, instead of coming here…"

"If you'd stayed here you'd be married, for sure," scolded an American friend when I was visiting New York a few years ago – and she spoke with authority, having herself been married three times. "You'd have found a guy who wouldn't be scared for his folks to meet you like European guys used to be with a foreigner. You'd be a lot richer too, maybe a name on television, maybe a novelist or something like that? You'd have been better off here, that's for sure, and you'd not have needed to write all the" – she hesitated – "the stuff you do to survive over there…"

"Yes," I agreed. "I would have survived easier if I'd stayed where I come from. But would I have lived better? No. I don't think so…"

"Expatriates' homelands soon exist only in memory," says Wisdom, pre-empting the last word. "And no matter how comfortably they are established in the chosen land, expats all know mornings when they awaken from the wistful dreams of a shipwrecked sailor."

14

I Told You So

"I always do my shopping here. The cashier, you know, the girl at the till? She always asks after my daughter. My daughter lives with her husband in Australia. Their father, my husband, he passed away six years ago. Yes, six years now I've been on my own. It's hard to get everything I need back home in my own basket," she said, nodding towards the far end of the till, where her own wheeled basket was waiting, "especially in wet weather. They deliver groceries, you know. But I enjoy chatting with the girls. It's mostly girls at the till, especially this dear girl… "

The bent old woman spoke to me as if to her own reflection in a glass. As is true of much aged agony encountered in my ageing life, she expected no answering voice, nor did she seek one, only a listening ear while we shuffled forward in adjoining queues at the checkout. Her trolley contained several tins, a head of cauliflower, a bag of potatoes and a carton of milk. She leant on its handles so it could double as a zimmer frame, the way her own trolley would later.

"I usually wait for this cashier, you know, the dear girl," said the old woman. She cast a silent frown towards the bank of self-operated checkouts nearby. "The dear girl is the first person I speak to on Monday mornings."

It would have been no surprise to learn that the young cashier was the only person the old one spoke to in a month of Monday mornings.

The aged are pioneers breaking a new trail to the eternal destination. Never in our society have so many of us achieved such great age and in relatively good health. And it must be said too that never have old-timers been as isolated within the community as we are now, so effectively ghettoized that younger relatives and neighbours can appear to be downright hostile when, for example, yet another radio journalist tells listeners that the old and elderly are a drain on the wobbling economy – as if our bus passes were as costly to the state as the mistakes and greed of international businessmen! And how often is it suggested, if not said outright, that the health service, to which a multitude of oldsters owe their longevity, is being destroyed by that very accomplishment? The old and ageing these days can feel themselves to have ceased to be individuals, practically ceased to be at all, simply because they have more time behind them than ahead. But wisdom is a gift that, if it is going to arrive at all, needs many a mile on the road before it finds a keeper. The wise respect individuality and recognize it too, no matter how unexpected is the source. Wisdom advances by way of observation and listening, and it can be difficult nowadays for us to hear each other or to hear ourselves over the drums of pedlars hawking flashy generalizations.

"I'm sorry to have to ask you this," say young voices at the other end of credit-card deals by phone, "but I have to ask your birth date?"

"What's so rude about asking a woman her birth date? Why does it require an apology?" Common Sense asks. "Do they apologize to men too when asking the same question, I wonder? And why should any man or woman be ashamed of the time they have spent living?"

"Whatever is expected to cause shame in a society," says Wisdom "defines its prejudices."

"I will not sacrifice my youth to my old age," I told my parents when they objected to my choice of being a worldwide vagabond rather than attending graduate school until a suitable husband finally turned up.

The young live in the here and now: it is more hopeful than helpful for elders to recommend that they consider the future before they fall in love yet again or drop out of education or over-invest their cash in a reflection in the glass. Nor is it constructive to tell them to stand back and consider where they might end up before they hit the road running. It is only after careers and families have been established that those approaching middle age begin to worry about how today's investments are going to affect tomorrow's returns. And for the new brigade of old folks whose tomorrows are becoming inconsequential and whose todays are emptying of employment or contacts with the outside world, it is yesterdays that return to stir their hours with recollections of the past.

Memory dulls in the short term – of course it does. Short-term memory is overburdened by an ever-increasing mass of trivia often encoded or requiring passwords to access, and much of it is of little importance to lives entering a new time zone. What's the date today? If you are not expected anywhere, if you have no deadlines or scheduled meetings, if nobody is going to miss you, should you fail to appear, what the hell difference does today's date make? What's my telephone number?

The first one was Delaware 3-6172; that was three quarters of a century ago, and since then I have had countless others all the way to the number of my current mobile phone, long and forgettable, attached to no address on earth. By the by, where did I put the damn thing? Never mind. I am not expecting a call, let alone a text. Nor does anyone expect a call from me. And so the faculty of short-term memory is naturally exhausted in due course, even if the wits remain spry.

"Can you tell me the name of the president of the United States?" the examining physician asked my Mother when she was deep into old age.

"That idiot!" Mother said. The doctor doubled over laughing and assured of her sanity.

Meanwhile, as today's details fade into the back of aged minds, long-term memory comes forward as more than just a motor faculty. The long-term memory of the old must qualify as a new emotion that is activated by advancing time. More instinctive than rational, although its effect can be displayed in words and pictures and music, the inspiration of long-term memory belongs only to the one feeling it. And as all other emotions, it delivers agony as well as pleasure.

Long-term memory can start torrents of words that listeners, especially young ones, do not care to follow. As often, however, those in the grip of memory enter a state of abstraction. Walking across an open space in central London, I look up to see green leaves against a pearly grey sky. The combination of colours picks me up all but physically to fly me back an ocean and lifetime to our "Victory Garden" planted against the threat of wartime rationing. In my pocket is a pinch of salt to sprinkle on the fresh-picked tomato I take away to eat alone under the silver birch trees at the bottom of the garden. So do we who are old or growing old fall silent, even among companions, when we are summoned elsewhere by the ghost of our younger self.

My mother collected memento mori; she even kept a human skull atop a bookcase. Her walls were decorated with African death masks, and occasionally she donned one before opening the door to a startled postman or delivery boy. Mother enjoyed shocking others with morbid overstatement, a lifelong indulgence that in old age passed as bravado in the face of death.. On one of my transatlantic visits, Mother nodded towards the top drawer of her dressing table and told me that it contained a hoard of pills to swallow as soon as she felt life needed an end. I said I perfectly understood, while silently I suspected that the old life-lover was having me on again. I found no pills in the drawer a few years later, when I looked for them after her death in a local hospital – a passing the attendant nurse told me was due "to age". But was it? Mother died while I was in mid-air, en route for a regular visit. If indeed she swallowed hidden pills and so made her final decision all her own, had she timed her end to occur before I could be present? And if that was so, was it to spare me bedside grief? Or to spare herself an audience for one performance that could have no curtain call? During a previous visit, sitting in silence with my mother, already into her nineties, the television flickering unwatched before us, I could tell that it was not dementia claiming her as it had my father – could it have been terminal boredom that sapped her energy, because boredom requires a present tense and it was the past that held Mother in its embrace? Memories were filling her beyond words, and melancholy though many of them were, they provided profound entertainment for her sedentary old age, and a distraction that she could not share with me or anyone.

"Are you OK, Mom?"

She turned her eyes my way, and the occupation I saw at work behind them makes me shudder now when I hear euthanasia proposed as a mercy for those who are assumed to be too distanced from reality to request it. I remember also sitting beside my father's bed in a geriatric care home, his present and his short-term past departed. He recognized me only as a friendly visitor. Befitting a dentist, my father's teeth had stayed intact, and his face sparkled with delight as he bit into an apple I had brought him. Would anyone deprive a child of such simple pleasure as my old father still enjoyed? Especially within families objectivity cannot be trusted: there are too many strings attached, tightened by opportune forgetfulness, knotted by pseudo-logic, or hidden below consciousness. "Past caring" is not a decision to be safely made about another – not by a relative, let alone by a professional whose main concern is the body. And on the other side of the humane token, should suffering swallow even the small pleasures of another, if they choose to put an end to what has become terminal tedium or unrelieved pain their last request deserves respect and assistance.

"Is everything all right, Mom?"

"It could have been," she said, and gave a laugh, quick and final as a full stop before her ghost reclaimed her.

"You've read about the divorce rate going up among us – I mean the over-sixties?" The woman sat next to me on the train. The article she referred to was in the open newspaper on my lap. "Oh my, do I not understand why! My husband

and I, we've been married for forty years. I'm sixty-four..."
she said, pausing to allow time to say she did not look her
age, "and he's three years older. Our kids are both grown
up and we have three adorable grandchildren. My husband?
He worked for an engineering firm. We had planned to travel
after his retirement – maybe take a cruise. I always wanted to
visit New York to see the skyscrapers. Well, it's been almost a
year. And all he does all day every day is watch sport on TV."

"He's bored? You're bored?" I volunteered.

"Bored! I wish! This is way beyond boredom. He's in a
different place from me. We're not really married any more:
we're flatmates. All he does is give orders about what he wants
to eat. If I try to talk to him, he's so grumpy!..."

Grumpy: the classic adjective for men of a certain age is too
low and monotone to describe the bad temper of many ageing
women, which tends to be high-pitched and on the attack.
According to one of the newspaper that thrives on dubious
statistics about our health and happiness, more women over
sixty-five are discontented than men of that age. If that is
true, it could be because many wives have the retired bloke
suddenly at home, ensconced in an overstuffed chair before a
perpetual screen and speaking no emotion beyond grunting
"I'm OK" to anyone who asks.

"It must be really hard... on him as well as you. Every morning for decades he used to be greeted like an actor coming on stage. His know-how and his competitive spirit were engaged at work. And then overnight, he's on the shelf waiting. You're right, it is beyond boredom. Retirement, for some – even those who looked forward to it – is a trauma in slow motion. You can't sit around waiting for it to get better. You need to find an active remedy. He likes sports? Sports are good. I mean to play, not watch. Does he play any sport? Do you?"

"We used to play tennis sometimes... that was when we first met..."

"Tennis could be a bit bouncy now," I said. "What about golf?"

There are plenty of people, not all of them females like me, who find watching or playing team sports a noisy soporific. The single time I actually attempted a kiddies' version of American baseball, my father was pitching, I was up at bat and my little brother was behind me catching. I swung at the ball. And I broke my brother's arm. Walking is my only regular exercise, and I prefer a destination or a purpose. But whatever are my own preferences, I have known numerous weary marriages among my coevals resuscitated by a sporting activity undertaken together, often along with others in the same age group.

"How about golf? Golfing clubs are pretty much managed by retired people."

"Not a bad idea," the stranger said. "The exercise would do us both good. There's a golf course that's an easy drive away from where we live. An easy drive? Is that a joke? I'll look into it. Anything to get him off his ass…"

"Once he's up and playing, you can make more ambitious plans," I said, adding the strategic word, "together."

"And as games go, there is always sex," Common Sense whispers.

"Or is there?" asks Wisdom.

Whatever the individual makes of aims and talents during a lifetime, the body assigned by nature is part of every history. The way men age cannot be the same way we women do. A woman before she grows very old is subjected to a rehearsal for retirement: the menopause. Whether the post-menopausal woman has children or wanted them, even though she has plenty of life and vigour to spare, a door has slammed for ever between her and youth: she is past it. With men it is not the door but the door knob that becomes problematical with increasing age. Even practice cannot keep an erection fit and strong for a long, long lifetime. Sex these days is recommended as a wholesome exercise for oldsters to indulge in, along with golf and swimming in lanes.

"John and I still have sex," an acquaintance in her sprightly seventies told me over a glass of wine. "At least we have a go at having sex every so often…"

Sexual play becomes friendly at last when it is shared by a pair of partners who have survived together through the best and the worst of it. Even if sex is less frequently undertaken and not essential to their well-being, at the very least it remains a nostalgic romp. Single old-timers like me and most of my single women friends gave up having sex generally when we hit our sixties, a conscious decision taken as more than one friend has confessed to avoid further hurtful rejection after what turned out to be a one-night stand with a younger or very drunk partner.

"Sex gave me up," is how one friend puts it, "when I gave up hoping for love. It was a lot like when I gave up smoking: suddenly there was so much more time in the day…"

"Welcome to the land of invisible women," Carmen said.

I was halfway through my fifth decade, and Carmen was a few years further along. Although Carmen's birth name was Susan, she exchanged it for the glamorous moniker long before I met her. Her daughter, product of an early marriage and premature widowhood, had flown the coop and wanted nothing to do with her mother. Carmen wore long skirts, high-heeled boots and beaded necklaces, and a long silk scarf always bound around her head with pink-and-purple dreadlocks descending from under it to her waist. While Carmen was living briefly in Soho, where I was then installed, we used to lift the occasional glass together. Carmen was self-employed: she instructed local transvestites on how to move with the grace of females.

"Invisibility is no bad thing," I said. "People reveal lots more if they can't see you watching them…"

"I don't want to watch people. Let people watch me…" Carmen said.

A bunch of builders were tearing up the pavement ahead. Carmen moved in front of me so we could walk single file on the allotted pedestrian passage. Looking up, the men delivered upon her the requisite ogle, followed by whistles that were not of lust but resounded with incredulity, a response which she preferred to the nothing at all, not so much as a second look from them that my passing received.

"Can you give me some advice? My mother is a real source of embarrassment. She wears clothes I wouldn't wear, and I'm just forty. She carries a guitar around and brings it whenever she comes to our place and, unless I stop her, she plays it and drowns out conversation. She lives on her own, and I really do love her. But how can I make her see that the way she dresses and behaves really doesn't suit an old lady?..."

"Your mother is a modern Amazon battling against the invisibility that age imposes upon women and men too, without wealth, power or fame to fill in for departed sexual allure. The way she dresses and behaves suits her. It does not suit you. Go online or check with a branch of Age Concern to find a group of ageing performers who need a guitarist. And if you cannot find such a group in your town, how about working with your mother to create one and put it into action?"

Mrs Wrigler was a white-haired widow who lived alone on a remote lane near our house in the country. She was seen out on Sundays on her way to church, and sometimes at the local store, where we listened to her talking to the clerk in a German accent that bespoke tragedy beyond the understanding of an American child in that post-war era. My friends and I used to hike past her thatched cottage for a look at the dozens of garden gnomes that were installed in its garden. Sometimes we glimpsed Mrs Wrigler behind a curtain while she observed our delight in her fairyland squadron.

It was the priest in our local church who noted her absence and called the local police, who found her body where it had lain for a fortnight at her kitchen table, head lowered into her last meal. The causes, Mother told me, were natural, only her lying alone so long before she was found in those days was still unnatural. It is becoming less so. Among the several oldsters, all but two of them women living alone in my own block of small flats, all have mentioned ruefully, rather than fearfully, the chance their bodies will remain undiscovered too, unmissed for very long by distant family members.

"And so," says Common Sense, "faith and churchgoing can offer old people a community and comfort here on earth as well as promising a ticket to the afterlife. It's shame that you and I cannot be drawn that way."

"An afterlife for us," says Wisdom, "one way or another would have to be an afterlife of agony."

Whatever is the destiny of classic agony columns which are already dwindling in print, whatever is the destiny of print itself, an agony aunt will ever be found sitting alone on the train or plane, some day on a space bus to Mars, ready to hear the troubled stranger at her side.